The Influence of Foreign Wars on U.S. Domestic Military Policy

The Influence of Foreign Wars on U.S. Domestic Military Policy

The Case of the Yom Kippur War

Robert W. Tomlinson

LEXINGTON BOOKS
Lanham • Boulder • New York • London

Published by Lexington Books
An imprint of The Rowman & Littlefield Publishing Group, Inc.
4501 Forbes Boulevard, Suite 200, Lanham, Maryland 20706
www.rowman.com

86-90 Paul Street, London EC2A 4NE

Copyright © 2022 by The Rowman & Littlefield Publishing Group, Inc.

All rights reserved. No part of this book may be reproduced in any form or by any electronic or mechanical means, including information storage and retrieval systems, without written permission from the publisher, except by a reviewer who may quote passages in a review.

British Library Cataloguing in Publication Information Available

Library of Congress Cataloging-in-Publication Data

Names: Tomlinson, Robert W., 1952- author.
 Title: The influence of foreign wars on U.S. domestic military policy : the case of the Yom Kippur war / Robert W. Tomlinson.
 Other titles: Case of the Yom Kippur war
 Description: Lanham : Lexington Books, [2022] | Includes bibliographical references and index. | Summary: "This book presents a comprehensive view on how the American military examined the aftermath of the Yom Kippur War and used that analysis to change doctrinal policies and equipment acquisitions. Ultimately, the learning that occurred as a result of the war dramatically improved quality and competency of American forces"-- Provided by publisher.
 Identifiers: LCCN 2022004048 (print) | LCCN 2022004049 (ebook) | ISBN 9781498568111 (cloth) | ISBN 9781498568043 (pbk) | ISBN 9781498568036 (epub)
 Subjects: LCSH: United States--Military policy. | Israel-Arab War, 1973--Influence. | Cold War.
 Classification: LCC UA23 .T66 2022 (print) | LCC UA23 (ebook) | DDC 355.00973--dc23/eng/20220131
 LC record available at https://lccn.loc.gov/2022004048
 LC ebook record available at https://lccn.loc.gov/2022004049

Contents

Acknowledgments	vii
Introduction	1
Chapter 1: A Brief History of the Yom Kippur War	7
Chapter 2: The United States Army and Its Reaction to the Yom Kippur War	19
Chapter 3: The United States Air Force and Its Reaction to the Yom Kippur War	43
Chapter 4: The United States Navy and Its Reaction to the Yom Kippur War	67
Chapter 5: Analysis and Conclusion	85
Bibliography	95
Index	103
About the Author	109

Acknowledgments

It is essential to acknowledge the outstanding contributions and assistance from those who allowed me to bring this work to fruition.

First, I want to thank my colleague and friend Dr. Jon Czarnecki. We started this project together. Although he was unable to continue, I owe him a debt of gratitude for his encouragement and intellectual efforts in considering the book's myriad elements.

To Dr. Gary Ohls, a retired Marine Colonel and professor at the Naval War College, who diligently read the entire manuscript and offered the best commentary I could have received. I owe him an enormous debt. Simply stated, Gary, you are the best.

To my other Naval War College colleagues and friends:

Retired Army Colonels Gregory Reilly, who read chapters and provided encouragement and sage advice, and James Adams, who provided expertise on the transformation of the U.S. Army in the 1980s.

To Drs. Craig Whiteside, Misha Blocksome, and Sam Helfont, thank you for your wise counsel and support.

Also to retired Air Force Colonels Ken Feaster and Clint Wallace who provided much needed encouragement during this journey.

To my children Katrina, Robert Jr., Troy, Tiffany, and Nikki, thank you for your support. Your encouragement for Dad is the important thing that motivates me.

Finally, to my wife, who is the best critic an author could ever have. I could not hope to accomplish this without your help. Thank you for always being there for me.

Introduction

"Why do militaries learn or not learn from their experience?"[1] This opening line from Richard Duncan Downie's analysis, *Learning from Conflict*, summarizes this book's executive-level focus and provides the springboard for a more specific application. What few books have attempted to ascertain is how peoples or nations learn from the conflicts of other nations. Specifically, this book probes how the United States military learned lessons worth implementing from the short, but intense, Yom Kippur War of 1973. The subject matter is a subset of a discussion on organizational learning: How do organizations learn and then use those lessons to increase organizational effectiveness and success? This book attempts to answer this question through five chapters. The first chapter is a brief history of the Yom Kippur War to give the reader context on the events that provided a learning opportunity for American military forces. Chapters 2 through 4 outline the learning experiences of the Army, Air Force, and Navy, respectively. They look specifically at the services' organizational history and culture and determine how those factors shaped their response to the Yom Kippur War. Finally, the book completes the case review with observations about what that learning has meant for the continued evolution of U.S. military doctrine in the wake of increasingly complex twenty-first-century operating environments.

THEORETICAL BACKGROUND

Research and scholarship on military learning is not new. In *How Militaries Learn: Human Capital, Military Education and Battlefield Effectiveness*, Dr. Nathan Toronto, former professor at the U.S. Army's School for Advanced Military Studies and the National Defense College in the United Arab Emirates, focused on military learning on the macro level.[2] His discussions of state power, civil-military relations, and the diffusion of ideas between states are certainly important issues when discussing military learning. However, such analysis does not cover how organizational processes within military services work to acquire knowledge and put it to good use. This study focuses on the organizational level of military learning.

Richard Downie, retired Army officer and PhD in International Relations quoted in this introduction, provided an important starting point to examine how organizational learning theory operates in military organizations. In *Learning from Conflict: The U.S. Military in Vietnam, El Salvador, and the Drug War*, Downie traced the importance doctrine played in successful organizational learning and change. Doctrine, for the U.S. Army, is the central idea or agreed upon concepts of operations within the organization.[3] Downie documented in his case studies that the U.S. Army could make significant organizational change through a learning cycle that included achieving organizational consensus and adaptation to novel approaches.[4] This organizational consensus, however, was often difficult to achieve and changing doctrine, which is the codification of organizational consensus, also proved problematic in many instances. He stressed the requirement to discard outdated doctrine to enhance organizational performance.

As a means of clarification into what this book will use as a definition for organizational learning Downie noted that institutional or organizational learning is "a process by which an organization . . . uses new knowledge or understanding gained from experience or study to adjust institutional norms, doctrine, and procedures in ways designed to minimize previous gaps in performance and maximize future successes."[5] Therein lies a distinct action-oriented component; information that is not converted into norms, doctrines and procedures fails to establish measurable learning. In this regard, the definition differs from more standard organizational learning definitions that focus on static changes in experienced-based organizational knowledge.[6]

Regarding military organizations, there are theorists who believe that such organizations are incapable of significant learning without experiencing direct trauma or intervention from their political leadership.[7] Dr. Saar Raveh, former director of the Israeli Defense Force's (IDF) Palestinian Arena Branch, chronicled in his article, "Why Militaries Struggle to Learn," that "armies fail to effectively learn because the senior command is conservative and attached to structures and doctrines that led the army to success in the past."[8] Yet, there are a number of scholars who would agree that military organizations are, under certain conditions, able to learn and implement such learning.[9] With reference to the current effort, Professor of Political Science at Barnard College Kimberly Marten, in *Military Organizations and Innovation*, concluded that military organizations are capable of learning and applying those lessons to doctrinal and organizational changes. She stated that "senior military officers are inherently reactive to military developments occurring abroad."[10]

The author's own experience with the military (twenty-six years Air Force active duty, and over eleven years teaching Professional Military Education for the Army and the Navy) plainly comes down on the side of those who argue that military organizations can learn. The stimulus of military failure, or outside civilian and political intervention, is not always necessary for this learning to occur. The author observed and experienced the military service transition during the Cold War environment where the competition with the Soviet Union spurred learning and change throughout the United States military. Circumstances within individual military services provided the impetus to learn how to succeed in relation to operational environments.[11]

Organizations learn primarily from experiences, directly or indirectly.[12] Here, the focus is on how military services learn from the indirect experience provided by a war in which they were not combatants. The main combatants in the Yom Kippur War were Israel, Egypt, and Syria; but both the United States and the Soviet Union supported their respective allies with significant enforcements of equipment and training. So much were the U.S. and the U.S.S.R. involved that they came perilously close to trading blows themselves, which would likely have triggered a nuclear conflict.[13] Thus, this conflict garners significant importance in terms of potential lessons learned.

The organizational learning lens used replicates Downie's approach but focuses heavily on Peter Senge's learning organization. The reason for its selection resides in its straightforward metrics for assessing the main question: Did the U.S. military services learn lessons from the Yom Kippur War? According to Senge, a learning organization is one that has the following five characteristics:

1. Does the organization apply *systems thinking* as a matter of course? Systems thinking is a predisposition to sense and act in internal and external environments using a holistic perspective, in which all the parts and functions are perceived to work and network together.
2. Does the organizational workforce, especially the decision-making core, practice *personal mastery*, or the process of life-long learning?
3. Do the individuals and the organization itself routinely question the organization's *mental models* or assumptions held about the organization that are critical to its existence?
4. Is there a sense of a *shared vision* of the future among the workforce of the organization?
5. Is individual learning accumulated into an available knowledge base that the organization can learn from, a sense of *team learning*?[14]

Organizations that routinely answer "yes" to the five questions above are thought to be able to learn, either directly or indirectly; organizations unable to affirmatively answer the questions are not likely candidates to adapt to changes in their internal or external environments, thus threatening their own survival.

The present book examines the Yom Kippur War as a significant event that should have triggered learning in the U.S. Army, Air Force, and Navy because the war happened across the respective environments, or domains, of all three services. This statement provides the operational hypothesis for the following chapters.

NOTES

1. Richard Duncan Downie, *Learning from Conflict: The U.S. Military in Vietnam, El Salvador, and the Drug War* (Westport, CT: Praeger, 1998), 1.

2. Nathan Toronto, *How Militaries Learn: Human Capital, Military Education, and Battlefield Effectiveness* (New York: Lexington Books, 2018), xiii.

3. John L. Romjue, *American Army Doctrine for the Post-Cold War* (Washington, DC: Military History Office, 1997), 10.

4. Downie, *Learning from Conflict*, 1998.

5. Downie, 22. [The approach is similar to integrating James March et al.'s "exploration-exploitation" tension that characterizes types of experience from which organizational learning evolves.] Read James G. March, Lee Sproull, and Michal Tamuz, "Learning from Samples of one or Fewer," *Organizational Science* 2, no. 1 (1991): 1–13.

6. Linda Argote, *Organizational Learning: Creating, Retaining, and Transferring Knowledge* (New York: Springer Science-Business Media, 2013), 31–40.

7. Kimberly Maarten Zisk, *Engaging the Enemy: Organization Theory and Soviet Military Innovation, 1955–1991* (Princeton, NJ: Princeton University Press, 1993), 3.

8. Saar Raveh, "Why Do Militaries Struggle to Learn?" *The Dado Center Journal* Dado Center for Interdisciplinary Studies, https://www.idf.il/en/minisites/dado-center/vol-8-the-general-staff-part-a/why-do-militaries-struggle-to-learn/, accessed April 1, 2021.

9. Not only is this Downie's thesis (read *Learning from Conflict* . . . especially Chapter 1), but it is the argument of most classic civil-military thinkers, like Morris Janowitz, *The Professional Soldier* (New York: The Free Press, 1960) and Samuel P. Huntington, *The Soldier and The State* (Cambridge, MA: Harvard University Press, 1957).

10. Zisk, *Engaging the Enemy*, 12.

11. Professor Jon Czarnecki, colleague at the Naval War College and retired U.S. Army Colonel, witnessed the rise of long-range (futures) planning within the U.S. Army, which had the effect of forcing the institution and its composite organizations to look beyond its own spatial and temporal boundaries to find ways to adapt to the fact of superior numbers of its enemy (the Soviet Union) on the battlefield. One

tangible result, as shall be discussed in the case from a different perspective, was AirLand Battle doctrine.

12. Martin Schulz, "Organizational Learning," in *Companion to Organizations*, ed. Joel A. C. Baum (Oxford, United Kingdom: Blackwell Publishers, 2001), 415–441.

13. William Burr, ed., "The October War and U.S. Policy," in *The National Security Archives*, http://nsarchive.gwu.edu/NSAEBB/NSAEBB98/, accessed February 10, 2017.

14. Peter M. Senge, *The Fifth Discipline: The Art and Practice of the Learning Organization* (New York: Doubleday, 2006), 6–11. [Virtually the entirety of Part II is devoted to communicating a deep understanding to allow practice of the characteristics, or in Senge's terms—disciplines.]

Chapter 1

A Brief History of the Yom Kippur War

On the eve of October 6, 1973, Israeli military forces set alongside the East bank of the Suez Canal and occupied the Golan Heights. Three major conflicts between Israel and its neighboring Arab states had reshaped the political boundaries of the region. Despite being the underdog in equipment and personnel, Israel prevailed in these encounters. The last, in 1967, proved a stunning success for the Israelis. The technological superiority of the Israeli forces and their strategic and operational acumen delivered a humiliating defeat to the military forces of its Arab neighbors. As a result, a virtual stalemate existed in the region for almost six years. Convinced that their principal adversaries, Egypt and Syria, had neither the capability nor the desire to mount an attack, the Israelis felt relatively secure across the barriers erected on the eastern edge of the Suez Canal and their fortifications on the Golan Heights. Yet, that strategic calculus proved faulty. In October 1973, one of the largest and bloodiest conflicts since the end of World War II unfolded between Israel and its Arab neighbors. This conflict would not only have profound implications for the region, but it would also dramatically affect how the United States military forces perceived future conflicts.

Numerous historical narratives of the Yom Kippur War exist, from the personal memoirs of politicians and military leaders to detailed accounts of the battlefield actions by those involved in combat. These accounts portray a chaotic struggle of high intensity where new weapons systems, manufactured in Soviet Union and United States, were employed with devastating effectiveness.[1] This chapter is not meant to reconstruct a detailed account of the Yom Kippur War; rather, it will outline the conditions prior to the conflict and reiterate how the actions of the Israelis and the Arab forces drew such concerted attention from the United States military establishment. Some fundamental assumptions in American military strategy and doctrine were shaken as a result of this conflict.[2] One example of this mindset change was the role of deterrents in conventional warfare. Prominent American military leaders and strategists purported that qualitative advantages in weapons and military training could deter larger, less trained, and inferiorly equipped conventional forces. For example, American military leaders believed they held a qualitative edge in training and equipment in relation to the Soviet Union. This was the same calculation that the Israelis held about their Arab adversaries.[3] America could not hope to match the Soviet Union in the amount of equipment or personnel, nor could the Israelis hope to similarly match their Arab counterparts. Therefore, it was essential that the smaller Israeli forces were more capable in military technology and training than their adversaries. As America's most important ally in the region, Israel had received the latest American military hardware and technology.

While this book focuses on what the United States military learned from the Yom Kippur War, it is imperative to understand that there was a distinct difference in the Israeli evaluation of their Soviet-equipped adversaries prior to the war versus the American calculation of the Soviet military. The lessons gained by the Israelis in their previous encounters with Arab forces influenced how they reacted to the events of October 6, 1973. The Israelis' overall disdain for the martial ability of their Arab adversaries had no similar resonance in the American military for their Soviet competitor.[4] This difference in evaluation criteria is valuable in considering the focus of U.S. military lessons after the conflict.

The Israeli use of western equipment and tactics, coupled with their well-trained force, contributed to a false sense of security. While American military forces were confident in their own training and equipment, the lack of direct confrontation with large Soviet forces gave them pause when examining the potential of these forces. Essentially, during this period there existed a greater propensity to change doctrine and tactics in the United States military than existed in the Israeli military establishment.

There is, however, a solid explanation as to why the Israeli military establishment held such a distorted view of their adversaries. From its founding in 1948, Israel had been in a continuing state of conflict with its Arab neighbors. Constantly under-manned and under-equipped in comparison to its adversaries, nevertheless Israel had been able to route its enemies in decisive military actions. At the conclusion of the 1967 Six Day War, Israel had achieved its penultimate victory, a stunning military operation that significantly enhanced its strategic position.

From the time of its founding the Israelis were concerned about their "strategic depth."[5] In essence, the concept of strategic depth is a nation's ability to have the time, space, and maneuvering room to react militarily to an enemy incursion. This reaction must occur prior to enemy forces seizing a vital area or infrastructure that would cause the government to collapse. Occupation of the entire Sinai Peninsula, the Golan Heights, and the former West Bank of Jordan (to include Jerusalem) finally gave Israel the strategic depth it long desired.[6] With its new strategic position, the Israelis were certain they could respond to any Arab attack and were comfortable that no further military or doctrinal innovation would be required to confront a major conflict in the near future. This, however, was not the case for their adversaries.

For the Egyptians, the outcome of the Six Day War in 1967 was unacceptable. In his memoir, the Egyptian Chief of Staff during the Yom Kippur War, Lt. General Saad El Shazly, stated, "The [w]ill was always there. Even during the dark time after our defeat in 1967, we sustained morale and spurred reconstruction by looking to the day when we would launch an offensive, either to destroy the enemy while they occupied our territory or to force them to withdraw from it."[7] The Egyptian forces planned to pursue this goal incrementally and, not long after the ceasefire of the 1967 war, began a concerted effort to confront the Israeli forces that occupied the Sinai. In April of 1968, the Egyptians initiated what they termed a "War of Attrition."

The War of Attrition began with an artillery strike in Qantara, northern Sinai. The attack left ten Israelis dead and eighteen wounded.[8] The Israeli forces did not sit idle after the attack and responded with an air raid which damaged critical Egyptian infrastructure and electrical grids. Between 1968 and the summer of 1970 this "War of Attrition" raged between Israeli and Egyptian forces in the Sinai. The Israelis continued to defend their forces in the Sinai in response to any Egyptian attack or ambush. The back and forth between Egypt and Israel on the Sinai front did not change the strategic equation between the two nations; however, it should have alerted the Israelis that their adversaries would not accept the strategic stasis indefinitely. In fact, both Egypt and Syria acquired a new ally for military equipment and training, which significantly affected the status quo.

The Soviet Union was a prime supporter of the Egyptian and Syrian governments for defense hardware and military personnel training. They hoped that their support for Arab nationalism would gain them political influence in the region and negatively affect the political fortunes for the West.[9] A 1970 declassified Central Intelligence Agency (CIA) report cataloged the extensive increase of Soviet military presence in Egypt and Syria after the 1967 Six Day War. Although the report indicated increased possibility of Soviet involvement in future conflicts, it went on to say that "direct participation of Soviet personnel in combat would not occur, or, if it did occur, that it would not be acknowledged."[10] However, the CIA's estimation was inaccurate.

Early in 1970, Israeli air attacks into the suburbs of Cairo proved humiliating to the Egyptian President, Anwar Sadat, and the Soviet Union. These attacks into the heart of Egypt demonstrated that the Israelis considered the Soviet-supplied Egyptian air defense no obstacle to their campaign of attrition against Egyptian military capabilities. This perception was particularly acute since these attacks occurred during Anwar Sadat's Moscow visit to consult the Soviet leadership about their military and political support.[11] After the meeting, the Soviets made the decision to provide more extensive air defense capabilities to the Egyptians.

In March of 1970, the *New York Times* reported large numbers of Soviet troops with Surface to Air Missile Systems (SAMS)-3s deploying to the Egyptian cities of Cairo and Alexandria.[12] The SAMS-3 significantly upgraded the existing array of SAMS and anti-aircraft weapons the Egyptians employed. Additionally, the Soviets sent Soviet-manned fighter aircraft to forestall Israeli air attacks deep into Egypt's heartland.

However, these Soviet upgrades did not deter the Israelis. In the spring of 1970, their cross-border attacks into Egypt climaxed when Israel conducted a comprehensive bombing campaign against the newly deployed Soviet Air Defense system.[13] As a result, Israeli actions against the Soviet-installed SAMS-3 became a key focus for Soviet leadership.[14] The weapons systems employed by Egyptian and Soviet technicians were identical to those at the heart of the Soviet Union's defense capabilities. Even then it was readily apparent that the exchanges between Israeli and Egyptian forces provided an important testing ground for Soviet and United States military equipment. The Israeli Air Force flew American-manufactured F-4 Phantom aircraft during many of these attacks into Egypt. Thus, the experience of these proxy forces proved invaluable to the Soviets and the United States as they learned the lessons of the Suez Canal.[15]

Three months after the CIA report indicated that direct Soviet participation in combat would be unlikely, a pivotal event occurred between the Israelis and the Soviets. In July 1970, in support of the Egyptian military, Russian pilots flew active air defense missions over the Suez Canal and engaged a group of Israeli fighter jets. Eight Soviet MiG-21s attacked the Israeli flight above the Canal Zone and a high-stakes dogfight occurred, resulting in five destroyed MiGs, but no Israeli casualties. The encounter between the Israeli Air Force and the Soviet MiGs had been deliberately orchestrated by the Israelis to teach the Soviets a lesson. Named Operation *Rimon 20*, the Israelis made the Soviets believe they were attacking unarmed jet reconnaissance aircraft before being ambushed by Israeli dogfighters.[16] The outcome of this incident over the Suez Canal underscored the predominant attitude of the Israel Defense Force (IDF) on the eve of the Yom Kippur War. The Israeli Air Force had bested the Soviets over the Suez Canal; other than the United States Air Force, they had beaten the best Air Force in the world. There was nothing left for them to learn when it came to air warfare.

Another incident described by author and historian Abraham Rabinovich in *The Yom Kippur War* reinforces Israeli disdain of its adversaries' abilities.

Prior to the Yom Kippur War, an Israeli patrol discovered footprints along a sand spit to the rear of their fortified position on the Bar Lev line. Because the prints bore the markings of Israeli military boots, they ascribed them to a wayward Israeli patrol, never believing the Egyptians smart enough to utilize Israeli boots to forestall their discovery.[17] Not ascribing intelligence, or believing their adversaries capable of learning new tactics, proved fatal to the initial Israeli efforts on October 6, 1973.

On the afternoon of October 6, thousands of artillery rounds battered Israeli fortifications along the Bar Lev line on the Suez Canal and the Israeli fortifications on the Golan. Simultaneously, Egyptian and Syrian fighter aircraft attacked Israeli military positions. Combined elements of Egyptian and Syrian forces, supplied almost exclusively by the Soviet Union, began an intricate attack crossing the Suez Canal and breaching the designated "Purple cease fire line" that had been established on the Golan Heights after the Six Day War of 1967. Although the Israeli government had not anticipated a major conflict against the Egyptians and Syrians at that time, they did have a well thought out contingency plan to respond to such attacks. The Israelis depended upon their defensive positions on the Suez Canal and the Golan Heights to blunt initial attacks followed by a rapid mobilization of their reserve armored forces, which would counterattack the Arab insurgents on both fronts. The Israeli Air Force (IAF) was essential to this strategy and critical in destroying Arab ground forces and ensuring the free action of Israeli aircraft across the length and breadth of the battlefield. Again, for Israeli military planners the critical IAF actions allowed their army time to mobilize and destroy the attackers.[18]

Later that day, as the sun descended over the western deserts of the Maghreb and the Mediterranean Sea, Israeli Air Force jets screamed across the sands of the Sinai and the hills of the Golan Heights. This was the pre-programed IAF response to any attack by Arab forces. However, that afternoon something new occurred. As the aircraft swept across the terrain to assault the attacking Arab forces, they were met with a barrage from ground anti-aircraft guns and mobile missiles. The Egyptian and Syrian gunners devastated the initial wave of Israeli attack aircraft. "The IAF, normally so meticulous and decisive, had been jarred into sloppy haste. In a single day, its reputation for invincibility had been shaken, a startling turn of events that affected the self-confidence of the decision makers and the air force itself."[19] In the first days of the war, the Israelis lost thirty-five warplanes.[20] This was a significant blow to a force that contained only 476 aircraft at the start of the war.[21] Other significant tactical blows would continue to set back Israeli military leaders' efforts to stem the tide of Egyptian and Syrian attacks.

The Israelis had installed an electronic intelligence gathering site manned by civilian technicians and a small IDF security force on Mt. Hermon, at the edge of the Golan Heights. Syrian Commandos from the 82nd Parachute Regiment assaulted the compound from four Soviet-made MiL 8 Hip helicopters. It took these commandos less an hour to overrun the site and secure a key installation in Israel's intelligence establishment.[22] Shortly after that attack, Syrian tanks and armored personnel carriers devastated Israeli forces along the Golan Heights.

The Syrian Order of Battle included 1,500 tanks and 115 artillery batteries.[23] The Israeli defensive position presented just two brigades of Israeli tanks, totaling 177 vehicles.[24] In the ensuing battle, the two brigades of Israeli tanks fought desperately against the overwhelming Syrian force. Despite the skill of the Israeli tank crews, the overwhelming Syrian forces exacted a heavy toll on the Israelis and threatened the strategic depth the Israelis had carved out during the 1967 war. The massive incursion of Syrian armor and artillery forces had pushed Israeli forces back toward the ridge of the Golan Heights. This was particularly true in the southern sector of the front. The potential for Syrian forces reaching positions overseeing the Sea of Galilee was a distinct possibility and a huge threat to the state of Israel. The rush to place more armored forces to stem the Syrian attack was critical. With the chaos and initial setbacks for the IDF, their one bright spot in the initial hours of the war was the performance of their naval forces.

The Israeli naval response in the Yom Kippur War was shaped by its previous actions against Arab forces during the Six Day War and its immediate aftermath. Israeli naval forces played an insignificant role in Israel's overwhelming victory in the 1967 Six Day War. "Outgunned by Egypt's Soviet-built missile boats," the Israeli Navy participated in only minor naval commando operations at that time.[25] They were also involved in one of the most controversial and embarrassing incidents during the war in which they, along with the Israeli Air Force, mistakenly attacked an American naval ship that resulted in the death of thirty-four Americans. Later in October 1967, after the war had concluded, an Israeli destroyer, the INS Eilat, on routine patrol off the Egyptian coast was sunk by projectiles fired from Egyptian Komar-class missile boats. The sinking resulted in the death of forty-seven Israeli sailors. These incidents helped to shape Israeli naval doctrine toward purchasing smaller, more capable missile patrol craft and instituting a doctrine of seeking and destroying enemy naval combatants at the first sign of conflict. This is what took place in the early hours of the Yom Kippur War.

The night of October 6–7, Israeli Sa ar (or Storm) missile boats sortied from their ports; one group headed north toward the Syrian port of Latakia the other group headed west toward Port Said in Egypt. Armed with Gabriel ship-to-ship missiles, the Israeli boats engaged five Syrian vessels off the port of Latakia and sank them all without incurring any casualties.[26] In similar fashion, the Israeli boats were responsible for sinking four Egyptian vessels off Port Said. The swift and dramatic action of the Israeli Navy ensured that Egyptian and Syrian naval vessels stayed close to their own ports and did not play any role in the conflict for the rest of the war. The actions of the Israeli Navy were critical because things were not going well for the Israelis elsewhere early in the conflict.

By the end of the second day of fighting on the Golan Heights, the Israeli forces that had initially engaged the Syrians were almost wiped out. Much has been written about the valiant efforts of the Israeli soldiers who fought against overwhelming odds on the Golan Heights. Outstanding training, unit cohesiveness, and a little bit of luck helped them in their desperate fight. In one account, members of the Israeli 188th Armored Brigade were scattered across a critical defensive line penetrated by Syrian forces. This non-standard deployment of Israeli armor allowed individual units to take advantage of terrain features to engage and harass the Syrian offensive, eventually sapping the strength from the attack.[27] The fighting took a fearsome toll on the 188th. Its brigade commander was killed, and the unit almost destroyed.[28] Yet, their efforts had provided enough time and space to allow Israeli armor and infantry reserve forces to mobilize and push the Syrians back to their initial positions.[29] By day four of the Golan Heights conflict, Israel had begun to reassert itself. The IAF had developed new tactics to minimize the damage inflicted by Syrian air defense batteries. In addition, the Israeli Defense Forces (IDF) employed combined force maneuvers, or the synchronization of armor, artillery, and infantry, which helped to turn the tide on the Golan. At the end of four days of fighting the Syrians had left behind over 800 destroyed or abandoned tanks and armored vehicles and Israeli forces were poised to move toward the Syrian capital of Damascus to end the war.[30]

However, in the Sinai, meticulous planning by the Egyptian military leaders allowed their army to breach the Bar Lev line. Within twenty-four hours the Egyptians managed to put 100,000 troops and over 1,000 tanks on the east bank of the Suez Canal.[31] Although the initial Israeli air attacks failed to blunt the Egyptian onslaught, the mobilization of Israeli ground units and reserve forces began immediately. The vaunted Israeli Armored Corps that so successfully routed the Egyptian forces in the 1967 war rapidly mobilized and assembled in an attempt to cover any breech in the Bar Lev line and regain the east bank of the Suez Canal. Yet, the Israeli generals' expected response from Arab troops to their armored attack failed to materialize and they were shocked and dismayed by what they encountered. When Israeli General Adan committed two armored brigades without the combined arms support of artillery and infantry formations, the results proved disastrous.[32] Egyptian forces on the east bank of the Suez Canal devastated these initial Israeli attacks. Egyptian infantry employed Sagger anti-tank missiles and rocket propelled grenades (RPGs) to wreak havoc on the IDF. At the conclusion of the attack, of the 170 Israeli tanks committed to the fight seventy had been destroyed and another twenty-five abandoned in front of the Egyptian lines.[33]

Israeli air and ground attacks persisted in the Sinai against the initial lodgment of Egyptian forces. However, the Egyptians' defensive lines remained static after the first days of the conflict. Gradually, the realization by the Israeli military high command and their senior political leaders crystallized. The situation in the Sinai was acute and the preplanned military responses proved ineffective. Eventually, it would be an error by Egyptian political leadership that changed the battle for the Sinai and gave Israeli forces a critical opportunity to seize the initiative and affect the outcome of the war.

According to Egyptian Military Chief of Staff Lt. General Saad El Shazly, he was summoned to his General Headquarters on October 11, 1973, when the "catastrophic blunder" began.[34] It was at that time the Egyptian Defense Minister presented President Anwar Sadat's desire for Egyptian military forces to leave their lodgments and press deeper into the Sinai toward two strategic passes, Mitla and Gidi. For Shazly, moving armor and mechanized forces from under their SAM protective umbrella to confront the Israelis in the open desert would spell disaster. Shazly warned against such actions prior to the initial attack across the Suez Canal.[35] The decision to move the forces was a political one.

Syrian President Hafez al-Assad exerted tremendous pressure on Egyptian President Anwar Sadat to find a way to alleviate the stress on Syrian forces because the Israelis were counteracting the initial Syrian success on the Golan Heights. The Israeli aerial bombardment and ground force maneuvers now threatened the Syrian capital of Damascus. President Assad pleaded for Egyptian help in the form of an attack that would force the Israelis to withdraw some of their forces from the Golan in order to deal with the new Egyptian incursion on the Sinai.[36] Begrudgingly, Egyptian military commanders ordered reserve armored forces on the west bank of the Suez Canal to move forward to initiate an attack on the two strategic passes in the Sinai. The results were predictable. Without their air cover in the open desert, Egyptian forces fell prey to the Israeli Air Force and tanks firing from established defensive positions. With a coordinated combined arms assault of artillery, armor, and infantry and without interference from Egyptian SAMs, the Israelis wreaked havoc on their aggressors. The attack, disastrous for the Egyptians in terms of loss of men and materiel, also offered the Israelis the opportunity to initiate a major operational maneuver, thus changing the entire strategic situation on the Egyptian front.

With the primary Egyptian armored reserve in tatters on the Mitla and Gidi Passes, Israeli military planners decided to conduct a bold operational attack on Egyptian forces along their vulnerable defensive lines on the east bank of the Suez Canal. The area, known as the Chinese Farms, formed a seam between the Egyptian Second and Third Armies.[37] The fighting at the Chinese Farms offered some of the most intense fighting of the war. However, the Israelis prevailed and broke through the Egyptian lines gaining a foothold on the west bank of the Suez Canal. Once on the west bank, the Israelis fanned out to sever the Egyptian force's lines of communications and dismantle the SAMS coverage that provided cover from Israeli air attack.[38] This operational maneuver gained the attention of the Soviet Union, who began to view a catastrophic Egyptian and Syrian loss as a blow to its international prestige. The Kremlin heeded Sadat and Assad's calls for massive resupply of war material and by the end of the war they had lifted 15,000 tons of war materiel to Egypt and Syria.[39]

After more than two weeks of conflict several things became clear to both the United States and the Soviet Union, the major suppliers to the war effort. Tactically, the Israelis had successfully blunted the initial Arab attack and gained a military advantage. The Israelis held a large enclave on the west bank of the Suez Canal and completely severed the line of communication from Egypt to its Third Army on the canal's east bank. On the Golan, Israel had blunted the Syrian attacks and advanced its forces within artillery range of the Syrian capital, Damascus. Yet strategically, the political landscape had changed dramatically. Arab forces had demonstrated their willingness to fight Israel and had exacted a heavy toll on Israeli manpower and equipment. Without the United States of America's massive lift of supplies and equipment to Israel, their tactical success was ephemeral.[40] The conflict had also placed the United States and the Soviet Union in direct confrontation. The Soviet threat to directly deploy large numbers of its troops in the area if Israeli did not halt its offensive caused the United States to place its forces on nuclear alert. This move signaled the Soviet Union that the United States would not tolerate unilateral Soviet action in the conflict.

As the conflict began to stall, it was American political maneuvering, particularly that of National Security Adviser Henry Kissinger, that brought Israel, Egypt, and Syria to a ceasefire. Finally, Kissinger brokered a larger peace agreement framework between Israel and Egypt that continues today. However, the carnage on the Sinai Peninsula and the Golan Heights drew tremendous attention from the American military establishment.

Many of the Israeli aircraft lost in the conflict were American-manufactured Phantom and Skyhawk fighter jets. These jets were in service in the United States Armed Forces at the time. It did not take long for United States Air Force officials to sit up and take notice of the high attrition rate of the U.S. aircraft due to the effectiveness of the Soviet-supplied weapons. In addition, the large number of Israeli tanks and armored vehicles destroyed by Egyptian and Syrian gunners were lost to relatively low-cost Soviet supplied Sagger anti-tank weapons and rocket propelled grenades (RPGs). Soviet soldiers would use these same weapons systems against American forces during any future confrontation.

Having recently extracted itself from the Vietnam conflict, and facing the daunting task of defending Western Europe from Soviet attack, the Yom Kippur War catalyzed American military and intelligence experts to rethink their doctrine and strategic and operational planning. The following chapters will assess how the different services in the American armed forces assessed and changed their institutional doctrine and structure based on their observations and analysis of the Yom Kippur War.

NOTES

1. Among the most prominent accounts are Abraham Rabinovich, *The Yom Kippur War: The Epic Encounter that Transformed the Middle East* (New York: Schocken Books, 2004); Lt. General Saad El Shazly, *The Crossing of the Suez* (San Francisco, CA: American Mideast Research, 2003); and Hasan El Badri, *The Ramadan War* (West County Dublin, Ireland: Hero Books, 1979).

2. John Mearsheimer, *Conventional Deterrence* (Ithaca, NY: Cornell University Press, 1983), 13–15.

3. Saadia Amiel, "Deterrence by Conventional Forces," *Survival* 20, no. 2 (1978): 58–62, DOI: 10.1080/00396337808441732.

4. Mearsheimer, *Conventional Deterrence*, 161.

5. Yoav Rin and Barry Posen, "Israel's Strategic Doctrine" (Santa Monica, CA: Rand Corporation, 1981) 5, https://www.rand.org/content/dam/rand/pubs/reports/2007/R2845.pdf, accessed April 2, 2021.

6. Williamson Murray, *Military Adaptation in War: With Fear of Change* (New York: Cambridge University Press, 2011), 268.

7. Saad El Shazly, *The Crossing of the Suez* (San Francisco, CA: American Mideast Research, 2003), 11.

8. Aryeh Shaev, *Israel's Intelligence Assessment Before the Yom Kippur War: Disentangling Deception and Distraction* (Ontario, Canada: Sussex Academic Press, 2010), 18.

9. "Soviet Policy and the 1967 Arab-Israeli War," Central Intelligence Agency, Directorate of Intelligence (March 16, 1970).

10. "Soviet Policy and the 1967 Arab-Israeli War," Central Intelligence Agency, Directorate of Intelligence, (March 16, 1970).

11. "The USSR and the Egyptian-Israeli Confrontation," Central Intelligence Agency, *Special National Intelligence Estimate*, no. 30–70 (May 14, 1970): 2.

12. "Soviet Troops and Missiles Reported to Be in Egypt," *New York Times*, March 19, 1970.

13. Chaim Herzog, *The Arab Israeli Wars: War and Peace in the Middle East from Independence through Lebanon* (New York: Random House, 1983), 234–235.

14. Herzog, *The Arab Israeli Wars*, 234–235.

15. Herzog, 234–235.

16. Michael Peck, "How the Israelis Shot Down Five MiGs in Three Minutes," *The National Interest* (April 26, 2018), https://nationalinterest.org/blog/the-buzz/how-israel-shot-down-5-russian-migs-90-seconds-25578 accessed April 2, 2021.

17. Abraham Rabinovich, *The Yom Kippur War: The Epic Encounter That Transformed the Middle East* (New York: Random House, 2004), 9.

18. Rabinovich, *The Yom Kippur War,* 33–34.

19. Rabinovich, 179.

20. Rabinovich, 179.

21. William A. Speier III, "Operational Art Considerations for Army Air and Missile Defense: Lessons From the October War" (Monograph, Ft. Leavenworth, KS: The School of Advanced Military Studies, 2003), 30.

22. Rabinovich, *The Yom Kippur War,* 155.

23. Uri Bar-Joseph, *The Watchman Fell Asleep: The Surprise of Yom Kippur and Its Sources* (Albany, NY: State University of New York Press, 2005), 213.

24. Rabinovich, *The Yom Kippur War,* 142.

25. Christian Heller, "The Impact of Insignificance: Naval Developments From the Yom Kippur War," Center for International Maritime Security (February 19, 2019), https://cimsec.org/the-impact-of-insignificance-naval-developments-from-the-yom-kippur-war/, accessed April 15, 2021.

26. Sam Helfont, "Cultural Challenges for Israeli Sea Power in the Eastern Mediterranean," *Naval War College Review* 74, no. 1 (Winter 2021): 53.

27. "Intelligence Report: The 1973 Arab-Israeli War: Overview and Analysis of the Conflict," September 1975, The Central Intelligence Agency, 57.

28. "188th Armored Brigade—Barak," Global Security Org, Israel—188th Armored Brigade—Barak (globalsecurity.org), accessed April 2, 2021.

29. Herzog, *The Arab Israeli Wars,* 320.

30. Herzog, 324.

31. Shazly, *The Crossing of the Suez,* 234.

32. Walter Boyne, *The Yom Kippur War and the Airlift that Saved Israel* (New York: Thomas Dunne Books, 2002), 56.

33. Boyne, 234.

34. Shazly, *The Crossing of the Suez,* 243.

35. Shazly, 251.

36. Rabinovich, *The Yom Kippur War,* 344.

37. In military terminology, a seam is often described as an area of weakness, usually found between two major military organizations. In this case the Egyptian Second and Third Armies would have slightly different command structures and chain of command. Such arrangements make it difficult to coordinate tactical actions by two different entities. Coordination for military actions in these areas is often difficult.

38. Rabinovich, *The Yom Kippur War,* 345.

39. Shazly, *The Crossing of the Suez,* 275.

40. Boyne, *The Yom Kippur War*, 105.

Chapter 2

The United States Army and Its Reaction to the Yom Kippur War

A historical examination of the United States Army just prior to the Yom Kippur War provides an important insight into the motivation for the Army's assessment of the war. That assessment had significant influence upon the U.S. Army's future organization and doctrine. Simply put, the Yom Kippur War was a decisive learning catalyst for the U.S. Army in its transition from its demoralizing experience in the Vietnam War to its reemergence as a powerful fighting force using a coherent warfare doctrine called AirLand Battle.

Founded on June 14, 1775, despite its long and storied history, the United States Army found itself at a crossroad at the beginning of the 1970s. Its involvement in the Vietnam conflict proved corrosive to the morale and the discipline of the organization. The American Army that planned and executed victories in World War II, and helped compel Germany's and Japan's unconditional surrender, found itself a battered and broken organization at the conclusion of the Vietnam War.[1]

The Vietnam War involved nearly 3 million American service members over the course of twenty years. In the end, America was unable to prevent North Vietnamese troops from overrunning the entire country of South Vietnam. Of all the American military services, the U.S. Army suffered most acutely from their involvement in the war. Soldiers comprised two-thirds of the 58,000 deaths in the war. Most were young men twenty-three years or younger; 13 percent were African American.[2] By the war's conclusion, the American people had lost support for involvement in the conflict and the predominately drafted Army was ready to come home.

After the withdrawal of its ground forces from Vietnam in January 1973, the Army began to focus on several issues that plagued their performance in the conflict and stunted their future capabilities. The low morale of rank-and-file soldiers, exacerbated by illegal drug use in the force, became a prime motivating factor for change. The easily accessible drugs in Vietnam ensured that many of the returning soldiers suffered with addictions. This affected the discipline and morale of returning individual soldiers, as well as in the other units to which these soldiers returned.[3] Given the well-documented social upheaval in the United States during the sixties and seventies, racial conflict and riots were also not uncommon on Army installations. Finally, the draft, which was responsible for most of the enlisted accession in the Army, was bringing in some of the lowest scorers on the armed services entrance testing.[4] Therefore, it was essential for the Army to reexamine its personnel system to recruit and retain highly qualified individuals to build a new, superior force. These issues were confronted by Army Chief of Staff General William Westmoreland during his tenure from 1968 to 1972. He was committed to transitioning to an all-volunteer force and increasing the attractiveness of the force to quality recruits.[5]

Although the aftermath of the Vietnam War proved problematic for the Army, its post-conflict goal focused on the institution's core values. A study conducted under the purview of Army Chief of Staff General William Westmoreland emphasized the values of selflessness, expertise, justice, dignity of soldiers, and physical and moral courage. This was to be the officer's creed.[6] By the mid-1970s, Army leadership attempted to inculcate the values of professionalism across the force. In addition to the focus on values and discipline, the Army placed greater emphasis on the major strategic threat to the United States, the Soviet Union.

This United States Army renewed emphasis on the Soviet Union directly resulted from the announcement of the Nixon Doctrine in 1969. During a tour of Asia, President Nixon met with reporters in Guam and remarked that the United States policy would no longer allow commitments in Asia to drag the United States into conflicts such as the one in Vietnam.[7] This was a clear signal to the Army that their time in Vietnam was over and the nation would refocus on its peer threat, the Soviet Union. This was an inflection point in the history of the United States Army. If the Vietnam War were no longer the Army's primary focus, dramatic organizational changes needed to happen to meet the new strategic paradigm.

One of the most important organizational changes to meet this new paradigm for the United States Army took place in 1972. Continental Army Command (CONARC), the headquarters responsible for all Army troops stationed in the United States, was deemed too big and cumbersome to carry out its responsibility to reshape and refocus the Army.[8] Army leadership decided to divide the command into two major headquarters. The resulting newly devised commands, Training and Doctrine Command (TRADOC) and Forces Command (FORSCOM), assumed their responsibilities on July 1, 1973. TRADOC assumed responsibility for developing and integrating Army doctrine, training force structure, and weapons systems, while FORSCOM would assume command and control of all Army operational units within the continental United States.[9] The Chief of Staff of the Army selected General William E. DePuy as the first Commander of TRADOC. Underneath DePuy, as Commander of the U.S. Army's Armor Center, was General Donn A. Starry. Both General officers would be key in helping the Army learn and implement key lessons from the Yom Kippur War. The critical geopolitical situation vis-à-vis the Soviet Union required the United States Army to learn quickly.

While the American Army was preoccupied with the Vietnam conflict, the Soviet Union had added more than thirty divisions to its ground forces.[10] These additional divisions, with new and improved equipment, gave the Soviets added capability to act against the West, short of using tactical or strategic nuclear weapons. Throughout the Vietnam War the United States Air Force and Navy maintained credible strategic nuclear deterrence against the Soviet Union in the form of land-based Intercontinental Ballistic Missiles (ICBMs), long range bombers, and Submarine Launched Ballistic Missiles (SLBMs). Yet, the United States Army did not consider itself a conventional deterrent against Soviet and Warsaw Pact forces. General Donn Starry echoed this sentiment:

> Visiting Europe shortly after returning from Vietnam in 1970, I found an Army in the field that looked upon itself as just a bunch of speed bumps on the way to the Rhine as far as the Soviets were concerned. They didn't think they could win. There is nothing more frightening than an army, the American Army particularly that thinks it can't win.[11]

The Army, as an organization, found itself in great difficulty during this period and its future far from certain.

Major organizations find themselves in trouble all the time. In the *Fifth Discipline: The Art and Practice of the Learning Organization*, Senge discussed organizational failure. Citing a 1983 Dutch/Shell study, Senge found that one-third of the Fortune 500 companies in the 1970s had disappeared.[12] The United States Army, however, did not have the luxury of declaring bankruptcy and starting over. Their ability to recognize the need for institutional change was critical for the nation's security. Institutions unable to change or adapt to new environments are susceptible to failure.[13] That is why as Senge emphasized organizations characterized by system thinking, personal mastery, mental models, building shared visions, and team learning are more resilient and less likely to fail. One catalyst for effective organizational change within the United States Army arrived on October 6, 1973, the beginning of the Yom Kippur War.

As with other U.S. military and intelligence organizations, the United States Army was surprised by the ferocity of the Egyptian and Syrian attacks on the Suez Canal and the Golan Heights. Within weeks of the war's end, Army Chief of Staff General Creighton Abrams dispatched Major General Donn Starry, his Chief of Armor, and Brigadier General Robert Baer, manager of the newest major weapons system, the M1 main battle tank, to Israel. The two-fold purpose of their trip was to acquire first-hand knowledge regarding the nature of the battles and witness Israeli Defense Force (IDF) leadership's after-action discussions.[14] Abrams instructed Starry, "I want you to come back and tell me what I, as the Chief of Staff of the Army, should learn from that war."[15]

The Egyptian and the Syrian use of Soviet equipment, and the horrendous attrition rate on both sides, did not escape Starry and Baer. If American troops were to defend Western Europe in battle, they would likely face similar attrition rates and intensity. Although the Department of Defense authorized the United States Military Operational Survey Team (USMOST) to gather overall lessons learned from the Yom Kippur War, Starry and Baer came to their own conclusion as to the lessons the United States Army should learn from the conflict. They took away eight major lessons:

1. "Modern tactical battlefields will be dense with large numbers of weapons whose effectiveness at range will surpass previous experience by nearly a magnitude."
2. "The direct-fire battle will be intense; enormous equipment losses can be expected in a relatively short period of time."
3. "The air battle over the tactical battlefield will be characterized by large numbers of highly lethal aerial platforms . . . and by large numbers of highly lethal air defense weapons systems."
4. "The density-intensity-lethality equation will prevent dominance of the tactical battlefield by any single weapons system. To win it will be necessary to employ all tactical battlefield systems in closely synchronized all-arms action."
5. "The intensity of the battle will make command-control at the tactical and operational levels ever more difficult. Radio electronic combat will interfere with effective command and control."
6. "The modern battlefield will require commanders to think clearly about some very complex situations; to decide quickly what must be done; and to issue clear-cut, simple instructions about who is to do what, where, and when in order to get done what the commander has decided upon. . . . Therefore, it is necessary that, to the extent possible, complex situations be perceived, solutions thought through, and reasonable

course of action postulated in advance in order to foreshorten the decision-making cycle—turning it, in time, inside that of the enemy."
7. "The outcome of battle at tactical and operational levels will be decided by factors other than numbers and other than who attacks and who defends. In the end, the side that somehow, at some time, somewhere in the course of battle seizes the initiative and holds it to the end will be the side that wins. . . . It is strikingly evident that battles are yet won by the courage of soldiers, the character of leaders, and the combat excellence of well-trained units—beginning with crews . . . and ending with . . . corps."
8. "Extended battlespace characteristic of modern battle demands the ability to 'see over the hill,' 'to look deeply enough into the follow-on echelons to find, target and deliver weapons against them."[16]

Starry and Baer summed it up this way:

The United States Army had to be ready to fight in the environment just described, fight outnumbered, and fight and win first and succeeding battles without sustaining significant or unnecessary casualties, and without having to resort, at tactical or operational levels, to the use of nuclear weapons to overcome disparities in numbers or other capabilities.[17]

Even though the post-Vietnam Army had already begun its task to reform prior to this conflict, the Yom Kippur War gave it a renewed sense of urgency. The Yom Kippur War acted as a real-time battle lab in which the American military could observe and learn truths about modern conflict.

An examination of the Army's institutional reaction to the Yom Kippur War demonstrated the use of systems thinking, personal mastery, the display of mental models, shared vision, and team learning—all hallmarks of what Senge would later deem essential for learning organizations. The United States Army recognized the need to ground their change process in accepted theory and called upon prominent social scientists and organizational theorists to assist in their transformation. This was never more evident than how they applied systems thinking to lessons gleaned from the Yom Kippur War.

Senge reminded us that systems thinking is considered the fifth discipline when examining organizational structures and management, as it integrates the other four disciplines, "fusing them into a coherent body of theory and practice."[18] Developing personal mastery, mental models, a shared vision, and team learning gains an organizational little without an overarching view of how they all interrelate. Training and Doctrine Command (TRADOC), the key transformational arm of the Army, was given the greatest challenge—to inculcate systems thinking into the entire organization.

In terms of systems thinking, senior Army leadership and TRADOC used lessons from several academic sources to incorporate systems thinking into the organization. First, the Army's Human Resources Research Organization (HumRRO) played a prominent role. The Department of the Army founded HumRRO in 1951 at George Washington University.[19] Its initial goal was to conduct behavioral research and training methodologies for major Army training centers. Composed of social scientists investigating human (soldier) behavior and complex systems, HumRRO assimilated the then-new research on systems training. HumRRO's systems training efforts focused initial attention on improving the effectiveness of the individual soldier; however, its scope expanded to incorporate more emphasis on the performance of the entire unit within which the soldier operated.[20] Eventually, HumRRO severed its relationship with George Washington University and incorporated itself independently to work for the Army and other government agencies.[21]

Shortly before the Yom Kippur War, the Army tasked HumRRO to conduct an organizational test of combat leadership formations. Dr. Joseph Olmstead, a senior scientist with HumRRO, conducted the study at the Ft. Benning Infantry School to determine why some battle staffs proved more effective in combat than others. The results indicated organizational competence as the principal determinant of a battle staff's effectiveness. Competence concerned the quality of performing specific functions and achieving mission-oriented goals within accepted organizational processes. When these organizational processes are performed proficiently, particularly under the stress of combat situations, an organization was deemed more effective.[22] This report, published just before the Yom Kippur War, was prescient.

General Donn Starry was already looking for ways to improve the capability of American armor forces, as Chief of Armor and the Commander of the United States Army Armor School. Capability and quality of performance were all things Starry realized he needed to improve within the armor corps. As he toured the battlefields on the Golan Heights and in the Sinai, and in his discussion with Israeli officers, he concluded that competent and effective leadership at all levels of command were necessary for an army to survive in modern warfare. He remarked that "battles are yet won by the courage of soldiers, the character of their leaders, and the combat excellence of well-trained troops."[23] This competence and leadership sustained the Israeli army given the overwhelming odds it confronted. A systematic way to train the United States Army to face the rigors of battle in Western Europe from an enemy that outnumbered them had to be developed quickly.

Toward that goal Brigadier Paul Gorman, the first Deputy Chief of Staff of Training and Doctrine Command, was credited with helping to bring systems thinking in the training of a force undergoing massive realignment and reequipping.[24] Enlisting another academic institution and organizational theory, Gorman initiated a two-decades-long research program that applied Massachusetts Institute of Technology's (MIT) Professor Edgar Schein's theory of organizational adaptation and learning.[25] Schein posited that all groups needed to adapt to changes to their external environment and adopt internal processes of continuous change to ensure the survival of the group.[26] Schein also noted that, as the world becomes more complex, it is essential for organizations to think systematically and "abandon simple linear logic in favor of complex mental models which will be critical to learning."[27] In conjunction with developing an organizational culture that could rapidly adapt to continuous change and new learning techniques, the TRADOC commander enlisted other academics to understand the complex nature of war and develop processes for better human performance in the form of battlefield leadership. TRADOC contracted with Dr. James Grier Miller, then director of the Systems Science Research Center at the University of Louisville, to investigate Army organizational effectiveness using Miller's Living Systems Theory.

Dr. Miller's background was critically important for his work with the United States Army. A Harvard trained psychologist and psychiatrist, Miller focused on human behavior and performance.[28] As a Captain in the U.S. Army Medical Corps during World War II, Miller was involved in "the psychological evaluation of field agents" for members of the Office of Strategic Services (OSS).[29] The OSS, the predecessor of the Central Intelligence Agency (CIA), required rigorous selection and training. Eventually, Miller's interest propelled him to theoretically merge biological and social science. His major theory integrated these two disciplines, which he expressed in *Living Systems* (1978). Miller focused on the processes of information transfer at both the organismic and social levels.[30] A comprehensive understanding of how people function in complex systems would be critical in ascertaining how the Army could perform optimally in a high-intensity conflict, such as it anticipated with the Soviet Union. Miller's theory would be applied as battle staff training and integration throughout the 1980s U.S. Army. Perhaps the most extensive use of its salient concepts was the case of III Corps, located at Ft. Hood, Texas. The U.S. Army's III Corps is one of its largest operational formations. During the period 1982–1985, under the command of Lieutenant General Walter F. Ulmer Jr., himself an innovative leader in terms of systems thinking, the unit utilized the techniques perfected by Dr. Miller in its battle staff training.[31]

The penultimate expression of systems thinking in the Army was the development of an Army staff specialty (50A) required staff course and handbook called "How the Army Runs."[32] This program, brainchild of Lieutenant General Richard Trefry (the Army Inspector General), applied systems theory to develop a life-cycle model of Army organizational processes. Early editions of the handbook included a chapter expressly devoted to descriptions, definitions, and technical systems theory terminology.

As the other requirements the Army undertook are examined, it is important to emphasize that systematic thinking made understandable the subtlest requirements in an organization.[33] The Army was beginning to understand the importance of all its members gaining insights on how the entire enterprise functioned. However, the broader examination of systems thinking within the Army concerned how they viewed their major adversary, the Soviet Union. Putting together advanced training, equipment, doctrine, and more importantly how they were to integrate these changes in a systematic manner to evolve would be key to building and sustaining a successful organization.

PERSONAL MASTERY

Personal mastery, a key component of a learning organization, promotes the discipline of individual growth and learning and considers individual competence and skills as key ingredients.[34] As the Army attempted to reshape itself after the Vietnam War developing personal mastery in its soldiers would become a major line of effort. Motivating and training new soldiers into their military specialties fell under the purview of Training and Doctrine Command. Its first Commander, General William DePuy, believed that the experience of the Israeli Army in the Yom Kippur War offered an important example the United States Army could use to develop this personnel mastery in its soldiers.

By the beginning of 1973, the Army was transitioning from a conscript force to an all-volunteer force and that necessitated a new professional training and education system. Military historian and professor Roger Spiller observed that the Yom Kippur War was "providential" in its timing because it enabled the Army leadership and the Army as an institution to implement an entire new and comprehensive means of achieving personal mastery.[35]

General William DePuy instituted performance-oriented training, which many considered a training revolution; this training emphasized individual and team effectiveness, as opposed to traditional drill and ceremonial spit-and-polish efficiency.[36] DePuy had been particularly impressed with the Israeli soldiers' training regime prior to the Yom Kippur War, and less than three years after the war ended, he made a ten-day trip to Israel. In a report summarizing his visit DePuy stated, "there is no other army like [the IDF], in the world. There probably never has been such an army."[37] The most important application DePuy gleaned from his trip to Israel lay in the careful approach employed to their combat soldiers' training. Tank crews were given extensive training to afford them time to gain the requisite experience before being placed in leadership positions. In addition, most of the IDF training was accomplished in the field, with realistic training and live fire exercises.[38] The trip helped reinforce DePuy's intention to reinvigorate the Army's training and evaluation programs.

From World War II until this period of re-evaluation, the Army's Training Tests (ATTs) system provided the basic mission and structure for unit field training.[39] Part of DePuy's training revolution included a change to the Army's methodology to outline and monitor training. The new Army Training and Evaluation Program (ARTEP) was designed to provide a setting more representative of, and attuned to, the stresses and complexities of the modern battlefield.[40] Under this new concept, the Army Training Evaluation Program (ARTEP) measured every task a unit was supposed to master in combat. One of the key differences between the old army training system (ATTs) and ARTEP was the focus on unit performance versus mission planning. Unit competence held higher value than how well its leaders had planned an action.[41] This was consistent with the efforts of Human Resources Research Organizations (HumRRO) who placed substantial effort into how units succeeded. Additionally, soldier training was oriented to performance to support individual success. ARTEP required a soldier to perform to a specified standard, not just put in training hours.[42] Finally, one of the most important changes brought about by the ARTEP was the requirement for certification of training by an outside military organization. No longer were individual units able to self-certify that they met all their training requirements. This was now done by outside observers and assessors.[43] All of these new training regimens were implemented with the aim of soldiers' personal mastery.

There was, however, another piece missing in the training regimen and in the Army's effort to achieve and implement personal mastery in its ranks. The home installation for most of the Army units did not allow for larger scale training ranges and simulations to conduct battalion-size training. Through an elaborate process of congressional authorization and funding, the United States Army was able to secure the commitment for the state-of-the-art training center at Ft. Irwin, California, designated the National Training Center (NTC). "Only Ft. Irwin had the necessary ground space for battalion live fire and opposed maneuver exercises and air space for electronic warfare and close air support training."[44] The NTC was an electronically wired exercise battlespace that featured an extremely realistic and competent opposition force (OPFOR). The Army secured approval for the development of the facility in 1979. In 1981 the first Army maneuver battalions rotated through the NTC. The facility not only provided realistic combat training but also eliminated a weakness in the Army's ARTEP by providing consistently reliable data on training effectiveness and performance improvement. Eventually, the U.S. Army developed other training centers to specially train other non-mechanized and armor units. These centers helped to solidify the personnel mastery of soldiers' skills across the spectrum of their required training regimen. Units rotating through these training centers, particularly the National Training Center, were observed by Army controllers who were experts at providing best practices and techniques to the units while also providing after-action reviews and evaluations of unit performance. These sites were similar in purpose to the United States Air Force's Red Flag training facility in Nevada and the Navy's Top Gun training in California. These training facilities will be covered in future chapters of this book.

The opposition forces stationed at these Army training sites studied and replicated Soviet tactics. Much of their equipment had been visually modified to look like Soviet T-72 main battle tanks and Soviet armored infantry fighting vehicles.[45] Additionally, the Opposition Forces at the National Training Center used Soviet-made lightly armored and tracked personnel vehicles captured by the Israeli forces during the Yom Kippur War.[46] Soldiers began to refer to the NTC as the National Trauma Center, as a reference to the hard and tough lessons they learned there.[47] The goal of the NTC was to have the units make mistakes there so they would not make them again in combat. Once again, as DePuy had summarized in his discussion with the Israelis after the Yom Kippur War, realistic training was key to survival on the modern battlefield. Yet, the importance of superb training and soldiers' personal mastery of requisite skills would not ensure victory in any future conflict with the Soviet Union. The United States Army still required a mental model upon which it could focus its efforts.

MENTAL MODELS

Peter Senge states in *The Fifth Discipline* that mental models "determine not only how we make sense of the world, but how we take action."[48] For the Army, making sense of any future conflict took the form of published doctrine. Army doctrine is defined as "the fundamental principles by which the military forces or elements thereof guide their actions in support of national objects . . . it is the body of thought on how the Army intends to operate."[49] Yet, before you can promulgate doctrine you must have a vision of where you believe your organization is headed. General William DePuy, the new TRADOC commander, laid out his vision four months before the start of the Yom Kippur War.

In a speech before his new command in June of 1973, DePuy remarked that the United States Army had to be prepared to fight against well-equipped forces that outnumbered them. The Army had to make sure that each American battalion was worth five of its enemy if they were to be successful at winning the first battle of the next war.[50] DePuy intuitively understood the importance of winning the first battle in a conflict with the Soviet Union. Any major conflict with the Soviet Union and the Warsaw Pact risked the possibility of one side employing nuclear weapons. Due to the fear of nuclear escalation, the first battle would be short and violent and American forces had to be successful if they were to provide their political leaders decision space. A loss of a conventional battle could quickly place western leaders in a critical position to either resort to the use of nuclear weapons to stop Soviet advances on Western Europe or accept their territorial gains.[51] Once again the Yom Kippur War provided an example of the importance of winning the first battle.

Initially, it appears counterintuitive to use the Israeli example in the Yom Kippur War to support the importance of winning the first battle. The Israelis lost their first tactical encounters with their Egyptian and Syrian adversaries. Later, they were able to regroup and gain a significant military advantage prior to the ceasefire that ended the conflict. Yet, the Israeli Defense Force's initial battle losses triggered a crisis in political decision making.

To this day, Israel jealously guards any information regarding its nuclear program. Their official policy is to neither confirm nor deny the existence of nuclear weapons.[52] However, it is widely believed by most intelligence agencies that Israel has nuclear weapons and the systems to employ them. These weapons were available during the early stages of the Yom Kippur War when defeat of Israeli forces seemed possible, and reporting indicated that Israeli leadership contemplated their use.[53] Although considerable controversy remains around the notion of whether Israeli government leaders formally decided to employ these weapons, the fact that they upgraded the weapons systems used to employ these weapons is not in question.[54] Israel had the ability to gauge the support of its most important ally, the United States, to ascertain whether it would ensure Israel's survival in lieu of its employment of nuclear weapons. The United States military and political support gave Israel the time and the materiel to regroup and turn around their fortunes in the war. However, there would be a different calculation for the United States in a conflict with the Soviet Union. There was no great ally waiting to come to the United States if it failed in its initial confrontation with the Soviet Union in Western Europe. The lessons American military leaders learned from this were that the loss of a conventional battle could quickly escalate between countries that had nuclear weapons.

The Israeli Defense Forces' performance and ability to win, despite being heavily outnumbered, resonated with DePuy. Their performance gave Israeli political leadership the time and space to make a different calculation, other than employing nuclear weapons. This is what the American Army needed to be prepared to do. To promote this model throughout the force, DePuy produced the first major Army operational forces doctrine in eight years. On July

1, 1976, TRADOC and DePuy promulgated and championed Field Manual (FM) 100–5; the core idea of the new doctrine was "Active Defense." The first page of the FM 100–5 states:

> Therefore, the first battle of our next war could well be its last battle: belligerents could be quickly exhausted, and international pressures to stop fighting could bring about an early cessation of hostilities. The United States could find itself in a short, intense war—the outcome of which may be dictated by the results of initial combat. This circumstance is unprecedented.[55]

This new doctrine gave the Army a new mental model. As the doctrine goes on to say, "The focus of this manual is to describe how the U.S. Army destroys enemy military forces and secures and defends important geographic objectives."[56] The manual emphasized that the biggest challenge the Army faced was in Central Europe, defending against forces of the Warsaw Pact and the Soviet Union. This new doctrine was primarily seen as defensive, hence the term "Active Defense" and focused on attrition warfare. This new doctrine championed the use of terrain and well-trained, well-led formations. General Donn Starry, then V Corps Commander in Europe, also supported the new doctrine commenting that the Israeli 7th Brigade was able to defeat the numerically superior Syrian forces on the Golan Heights by their excellent use of terrain and innovative and skillful military commanders.[57] Again, the Yom Kippur War was foremost in the minds of these commanders as they promulgated this new doctrine.

With this new mental model, the Army began a massive procurement program to acquire weapons systems that would help them execute their new doctrine. These systems were the Bradley Fighting Vehicle, the Patriot Air Defense system, the AH-64 Apache attack helicopter, the UH-60 Black Hawk Utility helicopter, and the M1A1 Main Battle Tank. Affectionately known as the "Big Five," all of these new weapons systems incorporated the latest technology to give outnumbered American soldiers an edge on the battlefield.[58] The Bradley Fighting Vehicle was designed to give American infantry increased mobility, protection from small arms fire, and a fighting platform. The vehicle offered a 25mm chain gun to support dismounted infantry.[59] The Patriot Air Defense System provided protection from high-performance aircraft as well as short-range ballistic missiles. These aircraft and short-range ballistic missiles were what the Army expected to encounter in a fight with the Soviet Union and the Warsaw Pact. The Apache and Blackhawk helicopters provided the Army anti-tank firepower and increased mobility throughout the theater of operations. However, the M1A1 Battle Tank was the key instrument for the United States Army to defeat the Soviet Union and Warsaw Pact forces in Central Europe.

Understanding the development and the production of the M1A1 battle tank is critical to understanding U.S. Army doctrine and its evolution into a new more comprehensive vision of how the nation would fight its next conflict. As the Vietnam War came to an end in 1972, the U.S. Army began its review of specifications for a new battle tank. Once again, the aftermath of the Yom Kippur War caused the procurement managers to reexamine the requirements to survive and win on the modern battlefield. Many of the Israeli tanks destroyed in the conflict were American-made M-60 tanks—the primary weapon for U.S. armor formations. In that regard, after the Yom Kippur War "the Army invested a lot of energy in gathering data on tactics and results, which were fed directly into the ongoing development of what became the M1A1 Abrams design."[60] The result was that M1A1 Battle Tank was superior to any previous generation of U.S. Army main battle tank.[61]

The most important advance in the M1A1 was that its improved armor made it more survivable on the modern battlefield. The new tank also gave the Army increased firepower and mobility. As the M1A1 came online and the other major weapon acquisitions came to fruition, the Army reassessed the Active Defense doctrine. These additional weapons systems prompted the Army to create a new mental model of how the organization would operate to defeat it major adversary, the Soviet Union. This new mental model was expressed in a revision to Army doctrine.

In August 1982, the United States Army Headquarters produced a new Field Manual (FM 100–5) and ushered in a new doctrine called "AirLand Battle." The new doctrine championed the Army's operational maneuver scheme, the basic doctrinal difference between Active Defense and AirLand Battle. Active Defense focused on an attrition theory of war, where the primary goal of American forces was to destroy weapons and equipment.[62] The AirLand Battle doctrine targeted the will of the enemy force. A major architect of the new doctrine, General Donn Starry stated, "the purpose of this whole operation is to wrest the initiative away from the enemy."[63] Starry credited the genesis of AirLand Battle to his time as the V Corps Commander in Germany from 1976 to 1982 and believed that the only way to defeat Soviet and Warsaw Pact forces was to move fast and strike quickly at the first wave of attack. However, to be successful, his forces would have to simultaneously attack the enemy's second and third echelon before their combat power could be brought to bear on American forces.[64] Despite improved weaponry, this could not be accomplished by Army forces alone. Starry recognized the need for detailed coordination with the Air Force to support this doctrine. This new mental model for the Army turned out to be a shared vision for the rest of the American military.

SHARED VISION

Again, Senge's notion of a shared vision is a critical factor for a learning organization. A shared vision "creates a sense of commonality, permeates the organization and gives coherence to diverse activity."[65] Shared vision focuses an organization's energy and provides an aspirational goal or direction for members of the organization. Shared vision also allows organizational members who previously mistrusted each other the opportunity to work in concert. AirLand Battle provided that shared vision for the Army and the rest of the joint force. However, this effort to share Army doctrine did not start with the announcement of AirLand Battle in 1982, it was cultivated by the Army years prior to that date.

As discussed in the previous chapter, solving the problem of fighting the Soviet Union and the Warsaw Pact on the central plains of Europe required a more systematic and holistic approach across the services. The initial steps the Army and the Air Force took toward a shared vision of the future battlefield occurred in the summer of 1973.[66] During a meeting of the respective service chiefs, General George Brown of the Air Force and General Creighton Abrams of the Army discussed how the two organizations could divide up the future battlefield to provide a synergistic effort against potential adversaries. Eventually, the Army and the Air Force reached agreement and developed the Joint Air Land Forces Application (ALFA) agency in 1975. Although the stated mission of the new organization was to "coordinate, integrate TAC-TRADOC programs for development of joint concepts, doctrine, and procedures for the conduct of air-land battle," the Army had other priorities.[67]

For the Army, ALFA was an effort to gain support from the United States Air Force for its new Active Defense doctrine. In fact, from 1973 to 1976 the doctrinal developments driving the TAC-TRADOC dialogue evolved from the Army's concept of Active Defense.[68] Eventually, the Army sought to gain acceptance and cooperation with its AirLand Battle doctrine from the Air Force. The focus of gaining this cooperation can be traced to statements by one of the biggest advocates of Active Defense and AirLand Battle, Lt. General Donn Starry. As the Commander of the V Corps in Germany, Starry sent a letter to the Vice Chief of Staff of the Army in November of 1977. Starry stated, "the most important perception held by the ground commander is of the insufficiency of air resources to help service the first-echelon army."[69] In this quote Starry recognized his inability as a ground commander to beat back an attack of the initial echelon of Soviet and Warsaw forces in Central Europe. Starry invoked an Israeli solution to the problem and said, "the [Israelis] have concluded that, for a host of reasons, they can't provide much if any close support in the battle against the first echelon. Therefore, they have decided to provide their ground forces with the equipment and the force structure necessary to make up the difference."[70] Although the Army was already changing its organizational force structure to give them more firepower, they still needed massive support from the Air Force. Again, General Starry championed the Air Force's role in this new doctrine. Starry commented that one reason he thought AirLand Battle was embraced by a lot of people was that it started out as a briefing and he briefed it to war colleges, staff colleges, and wherever he was invited to speak.[71] His socialization of the concept made the shared vision more powerful.

By May of 1981, the Air Force and the Army signed a new agreement on Offensive Air Support. This agreement provided air support by attacking enemy targets directly threatening ground commanders, such as enemy reinforcements and lines of communications in the immediate rear of the enemy frontline.[72] Later adjustments to this agreement gave Theater Commanders the overall responsibility to allocate such sorties, however, the Army had convinced the Air Force to accede to the importance of its priorities.

The Air-Land Forces Application Agency (ALFA) performed much of the joint doctrine development and initial staffing effort. ALFA helped to work through a plethora of service issues. Many of the policies that soldiers and airmen take for granted today, such as airspace control, air defense priorities, and battlefield and intelligence sharing, were formalized through the work of ALFA. More importantly for the Army, their acknowledgment of the Air Force's role in identifying and targeting the second and third echelon of Soviet and Warsaw Pact forces was critical to establish a joint vision. This helped to engender trust between the two services. Toward this goal Tactical Air Command and the Army's Training and Doctrine Command outlined the requirement for a deep surveillance and target acquisition system capable of detecting second and third echelon forces. This led to the development of the Joint Surveillance Target and Attack Radar System (JSTARS),[73] which was eventually developed as an Air Force E-8 aircraft with a ground attendant system that debuted spectacularly during the 1991 Gulf War. Army leadership understood that sorting out who would accomplish what role in this fight would require a shared vision and their relentless efforts brought that to fruition.

On April 21, 1983, the Army and Air Force Chiefs of Staff signed a Memorandum of Understanding (MOU) regarding "Joint U.S. Army and U.S. Air Force Efforts for of Enhancement of Joint Employment of the Airland Battle Doctrine."[74] The memorandum stated that "valid military requirements exist to initiate an agreement of inter-service cooperation in joint tactical training and field exercises based on the Airland Battle doctrine as promulgated in Army FM 100–5, Operations, 20 April 82."[75] After years of developing doctrine (its mental model), the Army was able to share it throughout its organization and with the rest of the joint force.

The United States employed concepts of AirLand battle against Iraqi forces with outstanding success during the 1991 Gulf War. Yet, it was not just systems thinking, personal mastery, mental models, and shared vision that transformed the Army and led to such success. The last aspect of a learning organization is team learning. Team learning according to Peter Senge "is the process of aligning and developing the capacity of a team to create the results its members truly desire."[76] It requires that the organization educate its members to think insightfully, to be innovative and coordinated in action, and inculcate the skills of continuous learning across the organization.[77] The Yom Kippur War provided perhaps the best example of the importance of team learning for the U.S. Army.

TEAM LEARNING

Army leadership recognized that the Yom Kippur War could serve as a powerful theoretical device for advancing its agenda of doctrinal reform and change.[78] The initial Yom Kippur battles had cost the Israelis dearly so, as the Army implemented change across its organization, the narrative it propagated was that winning the first battle was essential. This now became a clear focus for the Army. As winning became the desired outcome for all team members, they also realized that they would have to accomplish that mission while fighting outnumbered. In an interview, then retired General Donn Starry said of the new Army doctrine, "I don't think it takes officers, necessarily, or sergeants, who are any smarter than they have been before. I think it does take an early widespread and comprehensive understanding of the battle concept—what we're trying to do and have to do to fight and win outnumbered, particularly in Western Europe."[79]

When he commanded V Corps in then West Germany, Starry and his staff gained new insights into the Soviet Union and Warsaw Pact forces. He always pushed himself and the rest of his organization to find the best method to fight such a force if they attacked across the border. In a personal interview Starry tells a story of a visit he received from his friend and former head of the Israeli Armor School Major General Musa Peled. During the visit, Starry was alerted by his Corps' Command post that a major movement of Soviet armor forces toward the East and West German border had occurred. He and General Peled traveled to the border and observed that the Soviets had indeed moved an armored division, largely undetected, within striking distance of Starry's troops.[80] Again, Starry recognized this as a major problem. Such a large movement of Soviet forces undetected would place enormous pressure on the Corps commander. Peled suggested that Starry come back to Israel and revisit the Golan Heights battlefield for insight on how he might deal with a surprise attack of that dimension.[81] Starry did return to Israel and through discussion with that battle's commanders he was able to visualize and ascertain that critical vulnerability existed between the first and second echelon of the Syrian major attack formations the Israelis faced. The requirement to refuel and rearm in this space left the enemy vulnerable to attack. The Syrians dogmatically followed Soviet military doctrine, so understanding their vulnerabilities provided Starry and his staff new insights. Again, the desire to innovate and encourage others to operate in a coordinated fashion proved essential in the development of the AirLand Battle doctrine.

The Army inculcated continuous learning, another important aspect of team learning, through its training centers and its Professional Military Education programs. For an organization not known for studying or learning from its own campaigns, the Yom Kippur War provided an entirely new opportunity to put the concept of continuous learning into practice.[82] From late 1976 to early 1977 the Commandant of the U.S. Army Infantry School, Major General Willard Latham, traveled to Israel to engage the Israeli Defense Force (IDF). During this time, the Commandant met with the IDF Chief of Staff and other high-ranking Israeli generals to discuss training methods and new weapons systems. The goal was to identify and enhance both armies' institutional learning opportunities.[83] Brigadier General Paul Gorman, the TRADOC Deputy Chief of Staff, commented that working with the Israelis validated that the Israeli armor crews' training had proved decisive in their ultimate victory on the Golan Heights.[84] The TRADOC commander, General William DePuy, stated that "the training of the individual as well as the team will make the difference between success or failure on the battlefield. Well trained Israelis made the difference in 1973."[85] Their statements and professional observations make it abundantly clear that the continuous exchanges between Israeli defense officials and the United States Army critically supported its relentless drive for continuous training and education of its force. The U.S. Army's appetite for reforming its own training methods, equipment, and doctrine was quite evident as it invested a great deal of time learning from the Israelis.[86] The training centers from the infantry, mechanized infantry, and the armor schools incorporated these new lessons into their training programs.

As will be discussed in greater detail in the proceeding chapters, Professional Military Education (PME) is essential to American military structure. It underpins the character of the institution by reinforcing its core beliefs and traditions. Additionally, it sharpens the intellectual capabilities of its students by challenging old assumptions and emphasizing important lessons learned in military conflict. The Yom Kippur War also provided the Army Command and General Staff College and the Army War College a perfect case study to examine all aspects of a high-intensity conflict. The Yom Kippur War provided the Army's Professional Military Education system abundant lessons.

Army professional military institutions drew numerous case studies from the Yom Kippur War. As a professor at the School of Advanced Military Studies at the U.S. Army Command and General Staff College, the author conducted classes on the Yom Kippur War using Israeli and Egyptian primary sources. Indeed, the author and students performed field research and traveled to the Golan Heights battlefield and visited the Ramadan War Memorial museum in Cairo, Egypt, to ascertain lessons learned from the war. The *team learning* aspect of the Army emphasized information sharing, open discussion, professional dialogue, and senior leader engagement with subordinate organizations and units to communicate the shared vision to ensure shared meaning and understanding of the Yom Kippur War.

One key for professors of professional military education is not telling their students what to think, but to focus on how think and more importantly how to learn.[87] It is hoped that PME instructors will encourage their students to become life-long learners.[88] Professional military education helped to foster insightfulness and innovation and enhance the collective learning of the organization. All these aspects were critical to team learning for the U.S. Army.

In summary, the U.S. Army found itself at a crossroad at the end of the Vietnam War. Battered and bruised from the deleterious effects of the war, it found itself searching for a new identity and a new mission upon which to focus it attentions. Fortuitously, as General Donn Starry commented, the Yom Kippur War validated all the notions senior leaders held at the end of the Vietnam experience. The Army had to change dramatically to be successful in any future conflict with the Soviet Union and the Warsaw Pact.[89] As this chapter has shown, organizational change is difficult. For the Army, finding its way out of the malaise that affected it after the Vietnam War required a systematic, systemic approach and a mental model of improvement. Although the Army demonstrated characteristics of a learning organization prior to the Yom Kippur War, structural changes such as the development of Training and Doctrine Command and (TRADOC) Forces Command (FORSCOM) just after the Vietnam conflict helped the Army take a more systematic approach to rebuilding its organization. Key personalities like Generals Westmorland, DePuy, Starry, and Gorman played critical roles. They helped to spur the use of systems thinking and the development of the academic expertise to improve the effectiveness of soldiers and unit performance. Yet, it was influence of the Yom Kippur War that helped to transform the organization so dramatically.

From their tours of the Golan Heights and Sinai battlefields to their discussions with Israeli soldiers, senior U.S. Army officials recognized the importance for American soldiers personally to master their craft. This would be essential if the U.S. Army were ever to successfully survive a Soviet attack. The initiation of the new training facilities like the National Training Center in Ft. Irwin, California, enhanced that capability. Additionally, a close study of the operational factors that confronted the Israeli defense Forces helped the Army to develop two vital mental models—the doctrines of Active Defense and AirLand Battle. Active Defense stressed the importance of winning the first battle. As major modern weapons systems came into existence, the doctrine of AirLand Battle became the prominent mental model for the Army to confront the Soviet Union. The U.S. Army employed the ideas of shared vision and team learning as it used the experiences of the Yom Kippur War to convey its vision of AirLand Battle across the joint forces and encourage its soldiers to practice the precepts of team learning through training and professional military education.

The success of the U.S. Army and its hallmark of a learning organization was put on full display during Operations Desert Shield and Desert Storm. The Army that limped out of Vietnam faced one of the largest armies in the Middle East. Using primarily the doctrine of AirLand Battle, the American armed forces devasted the Iraqi military despite their sophisticated Soviet weapons. The successful transformation of the U.S. Army had proven their ability to learn from another conflict with devastating effectiveness. The next chapter will look at how the United States Air Force used the lessons of the Yom Kippur War.

NOTES

1. Richard W. Stewart, ed., *American Military History, Volume II: The United States Army in a Global Era, 1917–2008* (Washington, DC: Center of Military History-US Army, 2009), 369, https://history.army.mil/books/AMH-V2/PDF/Chapter12.pdf.

2. Stewart, *American Military History, Volume II.*

3. Stewart, *American Military History, II.*

4. On August 23, 1966, the Secretary of Defense announced a program to accept men formerly rejected for military service due to lower aptitude tests and disqualified physical standards. The program was labeled Project 100,000. The program was terminated by the Department of Defense in December of 1971. For more information see Rand Study, "Project 100,000 New Standards Program," https://www.rand.org/content/dam/rand/pubs/monographs/MG265/images/webG1318.pdf, accessed January 14, 2021.

5. Suzanne Nielsen, *An Army Transformed: The U.S. Army's Post-Vietnam Recovery and the Dynamics of Change in Military Organizations*, The Letort Papers (Carlisle, PA: Strategic Studies Institute, U.S. Army War College, September 2010), 37.

6. "A Brief History of Army Values," https://caccapl.blob.core.usgovcloudapi.net/web/character-development-project/repository/a-brief-history-of-the-army-values.pdf, accessed January 14, 2021.

7. Foreign Relations of the United States, 1969–1976, *Foundations of Foreign Policy*, I, 1969–1972, https://history.state.gov/historicaldocuments/frus1969-76v01/d29, accessed January 16, 2021.

8. Saul Bronfeld, "Fighting Outnumbered: The Impact of the Yom Kippur War on the U.S. Army," *The Journal of Military History* 71, no. 2, (April 2007): 469.

9. Bronfeld, "Fighting Outnumbered," 469.

10. Headquarters Department of the Army, *The Soviet Army, Operations and Tactics*—Field Manual 100–2–1 (Washington, DC, July 16, 1984), 1–1.

11. Lewis Sorley, ed., *Press On! Selected Works of General Donn A. Starry* II (Fort Leavenworth, KS: Combat Studies Institute Press, 2009), 1265.

12. Peter Senge, *The Fifth Discipline: The Art and Practice of the Learning Organization* (New York: Doubleday, 1990), 17.

13. Jeff Boss, "Staying Competitive Requires Adaptability," *Forbes.com*, April 26, 2016, https://www.forbes.com/sites/jeffboss/2016/04/26/staying-competitive-requires-adaptability/?sh=6d77a36c7e6f, accessed January 22, 2021.

14. Lewis Sorley, ed., *Press On! Selected Works of General Donn A. Starry* I (Fort Leavenworth, KS: Combat Studies Institute Press, 2009), 221.

15. Sorley, *Press On!* II, 1226.

16. Sorley, *Press On!* I, 222–223.

17. Sorley, 223.

18. Senge, *The Fifth Discipline*, 11.

19. "HumRRO: Who We Are," https://www.humrro.org/corpsite/who-we-are/our-history/, accessed January 24, 2021.

20. Anne Chapman, "The DuPuy-Gorman Initiatives," in *The Army's Training Revolution, 1973–1990: An Overview*, ed. Henry O. Malone and John L. Romjue (Washinton, DC: Center for Military History, 1994), 4.

21. Chapman, "The DuPuy-Gorman Initiatives," 4.

22. Joseph A. Olmstead, Harold Christensen, and L. L. Lackey, "Components of Organizational Competence: Test of a Conceptual Framework" (August 1973), https://files.eric.ed.gov/fulltext/ED080889.pdf, accessed January 23, 2021.

23. Abraham Rabinovich, *The Yom Kippur War: The Epic Encounter That Transformed the Middle East* (New York: Random House, 2004), 509.

24. The Gorman Papers, Paul F. Gorman Military Leadership, Collection: Strategy and Tactics for Learning, the Papers of General Paul F. Gorman, https://cgsc.contentdm.oclc.org/digital/collection/p16040coll10/id/99/rec/3, accessed January 26, 2021.

25. The best summary of Olmstead's FORGE and CARDINAL POINT studies can be found in Joseph A. Olmstead, *Battle Staff Integration* (Alexandria, VA: Institute for Defense Analyses, IDA Paper), 2560. Schein's model of adaptive coping is found in Edgar H. Schein, *Organizational Psychology* (Englewood Cliffs, NJ: Prentice-Hall, 1965).

26. Edgar H. Schein, *Organizational Culture and Leadership*, 4th Edition (San Francisco: Jossey-Bass, 2010), 73.

27. Schein, *Organizational Culture and Leadership*, 371.

28. Phillip R. Harris, "Dr. James Grier Miller: Psychiatrist, Scholar, University President, Author. (Obituary)," *Systems Research and Behavioral Science* 20, no. 3 (May–June 2003), https://go.gale.com/ps/anonymous?id=GALE%7CA102520659&sid=googleScholar&v=2.1&it=r&linkaccess=abs&issn=10927026&p=AONE&sw=w, accessed January 23, 2021.

29. Harris, "Dr. James Grier Miller."

30. Deborah Hammond and Jennifer Wilby, "The Life and Work of James Grier Miller," *Systems Research and Behavioral Science* (New Jersey: John Wiley & Sons, Ltd., 2006).

31. Colonel (Ret.) Dandridge M. Malone, "Implementation of the Leadership Goal: A Summary," *Army Organizational Effectiveness Journal*, no. 1 (1985): 8–14. (A summary article on the III Corps program.)

32. The history of the Army Force Management Program is described in detail in Gregory Lawrence Cantwell, "From Preamble to Foxhole" (PhD diss., University of Kansas, 2010), 13–48.

33. Senge, *The Fifth Discipline*, 12.

34. Senge, 134.

35. Roger J. Spiller, "In the Shadow of the Dragon," in *In the School of War* (Lincoln, NE: University of Nebraska Press, 2010), 232.

36. Spiller, "In the Shadow of the Dragon," 231.

37. Saul Bronfeld, "Fighting Outnumbered: The Impact of the Yom Kippur War on the U.S. Army," *The Journal of Military History*, 71, no. 2 (April 2007): 485.

38. Bronfeld, "Fighting Outnumbered," 485.

39. M. Dean Havron et al., "Improved Army Training and Evaluation Program (ARTEP) Method for Unit Evaluation," *Study Design & Field Research* Executive Summary, 1, Human Sciences Research, Inc., November 1978, 7.

40. Havron et al., "Improved Army Training," 7.

41. Havron et al., 12.

42. Anne Chapman, "The Roots of the Concept," in *The Origins and Development of the National Training Center 1976–1984*, ed. Henry O. Malone and John L. Romjue, (Washington, DC: TRADOC Historical Monograph Series, 1992), 7, https://history.army.mil/html/books/069/69-3/CMH_Pub_69-3.pdf, accessed January 29, 2021.

43. Colonel Gregory Reilly and C. James Adams, both retired from the U.S. Army, observed this first-hand as they trained their combat units from platoon to brigade-level formations. Colonel Adams also served as an Observer-Controller at the National Training Center at Ft. Irwin, California. Both are now Professors in Joint Military Operations at the Naval War College at the Naval Postgraduate School.

44. Chapman, "The Roots of the Concept," 7.

45. Anne Chapman, "The NTC Experience," in *The Origins and Development of the National Training Center,* ed. Henry O. Malone and John L. Romjue, (Washington, DC: TRADOC Historical Monograph Series, 2010), 86.

46. Chapman, "The NTC Experience," 86.

47. Colonel Gregory Reilly and Colonel James Adams, both retired from the U.S. Army, observed this first-hand as they participated in NTC rotations. Colonel Adams also served as an Observer-Controller at the National Training Center at Ft. Irwin, CA. Both are now Professors in Joint Military Operations at the Naval War College at the Naval Postgraduate School.

48. Senge, *The Fifth Discipline,* 164.

49. John Spencer, "What Is Army Doctrine?," (West Point, NY: Modern War Institute March 21, 2016), https://mwi.usma.edu/what-is-army-doctrine/#:~:text=As%20a%20military%20term%2C%20Army,in%20support%20of%20national%20objectives.&text=It%20is%20a%20body%20of,the%20Army%20intends%20to%20fight, accessed January 31, 2021.

50. Bronfeld, "Fighting Outnumbered," 471.

51. Bronfeld, "Fighting Outnumbered," 471.

52. The author has repeatedly experienced this during visits to Israel and discussion with Israeli political and military leaders about the existence of nuclear weapons and their nuclear doctrine.

53. Elbridge Colby et al., "The Israeli 'Nuclear Alert of 1973': Deterrence and Signaling in Crisis," Center of Naval Analysis [CNA] April 2013, 22, https://apps.dtic.mil/sti/pdfs/ADA579830.pdf, accessed February 1, 2021.

54. Colby et al., "The Israeli 'Nuclear Alert of 1973,'" 50.

55. Headquarters, *Operations Field Manual*, FM 100–5 (Washington, DC: Department of the Army, August 20, 1982), 1–1.

56. Headquarters, *Operations Field Manual,* 1–2.

57. Sorley, *Press On!* I, 326.

58. Robert Farley, "What If the U.S. Army's 'Big Five' Weapons Programs Had Failed?" *The National Interest* (July 24, 2020), https://nationalinterest.org/blog/reboot/what-if-us-armys-big-five-weapons-programs-had-failed-165555, accessed February 6, 2021.

59. David Trybula, "Big Five Lessons for Today and Tomorrow" (US Army War College, May 2012), 28, https://apps.dtic.mil/dtic/tr/fulltext/u2/a592510.pdf, accessed February 8, 2021.

60. J. R. Wilson, "US Armor Developments: New Technologies, New Environments, New Concepts" (Defense Media Network, November 13, 2014), https://www.defensemedianetwork.com/stories/armor-developments-part-2-new-technologies-new-environments-new-concepts/3/, accessed February 6, 2021.

61. Robert Tomlinson, "Airland Battle: A Doctrine for the USAF" (unpublished thesis, Air War College-Maxwell Air Force Base, AL, January 1992), 6.

62. Jeffrey Long, "The Evolution of U.S. Army Doctrine, From Active Defense to Airland Battle and Beyond" (Thesis for Master of Military Art and Science, Ft. Leavenworth, KS, 1991), 31.

63. Sorley, *Press On!* I, 376.

64. Sorley, 374.

65. Senge, *The Fifth Discipline,* 192.

66. Richard G. Davis, "The 31 Initiatives: A Study in Air Force-Army Cooperation" (Washington, DC: Office of Air Force History, 1987), 25.

67. Dana Smith, "The Air Land Sea Application Center Commemorates 40 Years," *Air Land Sea Bulletin*, no. 2015-3, Air Land Sea Application Center (July 2015).

68. Davis, "The 31 Initiatives," 27.

69. Sorley, *Press On!* I, 2.

70. Sorley, 2.

71. Sorley, *Press On!* II, 1275.

72. Davis, "The 31 Initiatives," 30.

73. Sorley, *Press On!* I, xvi.

74. Davis, "The 31 Initiatives," 91.

75. Davis, 30.

76. Senge, *The Fifth Discipline*, 218.

77. Senge, 219.

78. R. Z. Alessi-Friedlander, "Learning to Win While Fighting Outnumbered: General Donn A. Starry and the Challenge of Institutional Leadership during a Period of Reform and Modernization," *Military Review* Online Exclusive (April 2017), Learning to Win While Fighting Outnumbered (army.mil), accessed February 16, 2021.

79. Sorely, *Press On!* II, 1220.

80. Sorley, 1285.

81. Sorley, 1285.

82. Ethan Orwin, "Not an Intellectual Exercise: Lessons from U.S.-Israeli Institutional Army Cooperation, 1973–1982," *Military ReviewWar,* Ft. Leavenworth, KS, Army University Press (January–February 2020): 49.

83. Orwin, "Not an Intellectual Exercise," 47.

84. Orwin, 49.

85. David Rodman, "Eagle's Eye View: An American Assessment of the 1973 Yom Kippur War," *Intelligence and National Security Journal* (March 5, 2015).

86. Orwin, "Not an Intellectual Exercise," 48.

87. Bradley Carter, "No 'Holidays from History': Adult Learning, Professional Military Education, and Teaching History," *Military Culture and History* I, ed. Douglas Higbee (Surrey, England: Ashgate Publishing, 2010), 170.

88. The author has attended PME in residence at intermediate and senior levels and has taught at both levels for over a decade. He has observed the goal of PME instruction and the end product of the instruction.

89. Sorley, *Press On!* II, 1109.

Chapter 3

The United States Air Force and Its Reaction to the Yom Kippur War

To fully comprehend the United States Air Force's reaction to the Yom Kippur War, it is vital to understand how its origins inform and influence its organizational culture. From its beginnings, the Air Force operated in a domain that heretofore had been unavailable to military forces. Its operations in this new domain fostered a unique approach to problem solving and organizational culture, which directly impacted its course of action after the end of the Yom Kippur War.

THE UNITED STATES AIR FORCE PRIOR TO THE YOM KIPPUR WAR

As the youngest of the American armed forces covered in this book, the United States Air Force was hewn from the structure of the United States Army. From its beginnings in 1907 as the Air Service of the Army Signal Corps to the powerful United States Army Air Forces (USAAF) at the end of World War II, American airmen wrestled with discovering the best military use for the new technology of aircraft. Within the Army Air Service, later the Army Air Corps, leadership worried about the development and organization of aircraft units for military purposes because they believed the Army's organizational structure inhibited and underfunded the development of airpower.[1] Even at the end of World War II, where military aviation had proven itself a vital component of American success, airmen still longed for the day when airpower would be extricated from the purview of the United States Army. Their most fervent desire was to have the air force recognized as an independent service.[2] In September 1947, U.S. airmen were granted their wish. The

National Defense Reorganizational Act of 1947 designated the United States Air Force a separate armed service. This important action allowed airmen to develop their own doctrine, train their own forces, and acquire and purchase their own equipment.

From its inception as a separate service, the United States Air Force attempted to harness new technology and develop organizational practices to unleash the capabilities of airpower. Effective strategic bombing and the employment of massive numbers of tactical aircraft in World War II proved a mere starting point for the service.[3] The new United States Air Force leaders understood that aircraft were essentially an expression of the miracles of technology.[4] The Air Force continued to leverage that technology by developing new procedures and perfecting equipment that enhanced the capabilities of military airpower. The combined efforts of airmen, industry, and technologists resulted in spectacular aviation achievements. The development of air-to-air refueling, intercontinental strategic bombers, and intercontinental ballistic missiles (ICBMs) comprise only a few of the numerous Air Force accomplishments. Additionally, the Air Force demonstrated its ability to use airpower in a non-lethal manner by perfecting its ability to perform strategic airlift of supplies and equipment globally. There was no more poignant example of that capability than the famous Berlin Airlift beginning June 26, 1948.

At the conclusion of World War II America, Great Britain, and France shared the occupation of the former Nazi capital of Berlin with the Soviet Union, yet the Soviet Union controlled all land access to the city through the territory it occupied in Germany. The Soviets blocked all land resupply routes to Western Berlin in an attempt to squeeze the Americans and their allies out of the capital. In concert with the rest of the allies, the nascent United States Air Force organized a fifteen-month aerial resupply campaign of West Berlin (Operation Vittles). This resupply effort included lifesaving supplies and equipment to support the city's civilian population and allied forces during the Soviet and Warsaw Pact blockade. In the end, this joint action proved decisive in changing the behavior of the Soviet Union toward allied forces in Berlin.[5]

Operation Vittles' success and the continued development of airpower in the late 1940s through the early part of the 1970s proved significant for the United States Air Force. It demonstrated organizational capability to innovate and develop new concepts to solve problems. Yet, in the two major post–World War II conflicts, the United States Air Force failed to be a decisive factor in ending the war to the United States' advantage. As an organization, the United States Air Force attempted to examine its role in those conflicts to discern how to achieve its commitment to support American defense policy more effectively.

In the Korean War, the first major conflict after World War II, the United States responded to an overwhelming attack by North Korean forces determined to take over South Korea. American air forces acquitted themselves well against Soviet-made North Korean aircraft during their early commitment to the war.[6] The U.S. Air Force's major goal of air superiority above South Korea would allow United Nations ground forces greater freedom to oppose the more powerful North Korean ground forces. Within the first few weeks of the conflict the United States Air Force accomplished that goal.[7] The United States Air Force also conducted interdiction missions, which consisted of destroying communication lines, equipment, and supplies from bases in North Korea in route to their forces in the field. Additionally, the Air Force involved itself in the close air support mission, directly supporting forces in contact with the enemy with bombing and strafing missions.

Surprisingly, the close air support mission initially proved problematic for the United States Air Force. Close air support, one of the core missions of tactical airpower, exposed a lack of synergistic cooperation between Army and Air Force doctrine. The United States Marine Corps' air capabilities afforded it a better opportunity to support troops in contact.[8] Forged during its island-hopping campaign in the Pacific during World War II, Marine Corps aviation possesses a deep historical and practical association in supporting its ground maneuver elements. The Marine Corps specifically structured its aviation capability to support its ground maneuver elements due to the lack of organic artillery during its Pacific island campaign. Thus, Marine aviators' experiences in World War II enabled them to achieve the requisite expertise to skillfully support their ground troops.[9]

Eventually, the United States Air Force coordinated with the Army to organize and employ tactical control groups and develop the necessary communication systems to bolster the close air support mission. These newly differentiated organizations developed a more effective method to employ airpower to support ground forces in contact with North Korean troops.[10] A more effective close air support and command and control apparatus allowed American and allied forces to push the North Korean forces back into North Korea and close to the Yalu River, the boundary between China and North Korea. As American ground forces approached the Yalu River, a new and more daunting challenge faced the Air Force—the direct intervention of Chinese forces into the conflict. By November of 1950 it was estimated that over 300,000 Chinese troops had entered the conflict in support of the North Koreans with the stated purpose of pushing all United States and allied personnel out of North Korea.

Because American political leaders prohibited pilots from entering Chinese airspace, the Air Force now faced the additional complication of North Korean and Chinese pilots flying from their sanctuary in Manchuria, China.

These confrontations over North Korea were strictly air-to-air engagements without the political clearance to destroy the adversaries' equipment on the ground. As more advanced Soviet-made fighter aircraft became available to North Korean and Chinese pilots, the requirement to design and build faster and better aircraft was particularly acute for the U.S. Air Force.[11]

The ability of airmen to recognize requirements and establish new materiel needs was important. However, the lag time from need to production was certainly eye opening. In 1950, most of the required aircraft and fixes never made it into production before the war's end.[12] When the Koreas signed the eventual armistice, both sides agreed to establish a Demilitarized Zone (DMZ) at the 38th parallel, roughly the same boundary between North and South Korea before the war. Although the United States Air Force had proven itself essential to the war effort, the outcome had not been decisive. Airmen continued to review their capabilities and organizational structures to prepare to resist the global communist threat.[13] It would not take long for that new threat to emerge.

America's involvement in Vietnam began gradually with support for the French government's attempt to maintain its Indochina colony in the 1950s. Eventually, although officially undeclared, the conflict would evolve into one of America's bloodiest wars. By the end of the conflict, many motives undergirded the United States Air Forces' necessity to reevaluate and scrutinize its capabilities and effectiveness. This tougher scrutiny had many causal reasons, not the least of which was the ultimate political outcome of the war. The United States withdrew from South Vietnam after achieving none of its major political goals. In the end, the North Vietnamese communist regime successfully defeated the South Vietnamese military force and unified the country under North Vietnam's leadership.

During the conflict, the United States Air Force committed an enormous array of force structure and aircraft to defeat North Vietnam and the Communist insurgents in South Vietnam (the Viet Cong). Airpower theorists, who had postulated the supremacy of U.S. air power in war, had to reevaluate their theories.[14] The assumption that bombing North Vietnam would boost South Vietnamese morale and break the will of the North proved faulty.[15] Although successful in air-to-air engagements, close air support, sustainment, and resupply of global forces, once again the full promise of airpower went unrealized. Despite the U.S. use of strategic bombers and fighter aircraft for battlefield air interdiction, the North Vietnamese continued their campaign against the South. According to the National Archives, the U.S. Air Force lost 2,250 aircraft and 2,586 American airmen during the Vietnam War.[16] This was a significant price for failure.

As Benjamin Lambeth states in his book *The Transformation of American Air Power*, "[T]he Vietnam War was a defining experience for American airpower . . . the air war over North Vietnam highlighted a number of emerging problems associated with conducting modern conventional war against a well-equipped and sophisticated opponent."[17] Although the Air Force demonstrated characteristics of what organizational guru and author Peter Senge applied to a learning organization from its inception, such trends were accelerated in the aftermath of the Vietnam War. Since that time, the Air Force continued to develop and implement the very characteristics Senge identified in learning organizations—systems thinking, personal mastery, mental models, shared vision, and team learning. How the Air Force dealt with the aftermath of the Yom Kippur War clearly demonstrated the service as a learning organization.

HOW THE AIR FORCE VIEWED THE YOM KIPPUR WAR

The Yom Kippur War almost immediately impacted the United States Air Force. At the start of the war, the 9th Strategic Reconnaissance Wing, at Beale Air Force Base, California, was alerted to deploy its SR-71A strategic reconnaissance aircraft to survey the battlefield in real time.[18] Flying at over Mach 3.5 with an altitude ceiling of 80,000 feet, the warring parties had little chance to intercept the aircraft. This approach enabled the aircraft to acquire and provide real-time situational intelligence. Based upon the reconnaissance and Israeli government communication, American political leaders quickly assessed that the Israelis required immediate assistance to urgently replace fighter aircraft and air-to-air missiles.

On October 13, 1973, the United States Air Force launched one of the largest resupply efforts since the Berlin Airlift. Operation Nickel Grass delivered much needed supplies and equipment to the Israeli forces. The Air Force also transferred over forty F-4 aircraft from its active inventory to replace Israeli aircraft lost in the war.[19] By the war's conclusion, the U.S. Air Force had already learned direct lessons; meticulous after-action review resulted in many more.

Perhaps the two best accounts of how the United States Air Force reacted in the aftermath of the Yom Kippur War are covered by a publication from the School of Advanced Aerospace Studies by Joseph S. Doyle of the Royal Air Force and a thesis from Trevor Cutler from the University of Calgary. Worthy of investigation, both papers outlined in detail how the Air Force initiated research and training after the Yom Kippur War.[20] Yet, to fully appreciate whether the Air Force exhibited the characteristics of a learning organization requires deeper analysis. It is instructive that the United States Department of Defense and the United States Air Force recognized instructive opportunities soon after the conflict's conclusion.

OUTLINING THE CHALLENGES

Soon after the Yom Kippur War ended, the Department of Defense directed an assessment of the military ramifications. Secretary of Defense James Schlesinger ordered the formation of a fact finding United States Military Operational Survey Team (USMOST) and directed the United States Air Force, along with the other military services and defense agencies, to collaborate and gain first-hand operational lessons from the Yom Kippur War.[21] The team traveled to Israel to ascertain how Soviet- and American-made equipment performed on the battlefield and secured Soviet equipment captured by the Israelis for shipment back to America.[22]

Beyond the USMOST mandate, the Air Force undertook an independent initiative to analyze the results of the war and incorporate lessons learned. This initiative, directed by Secretary of the Air Force John McLucas, sought to ensure that all future Air Force programs inculcated the most significant lessons from the war into planning, budgeting, training, and deployment considerations.[23] The top service leadership also pursued meetings with their Israeli counterparts. In March of 1974, General Robert J. Dixon, Commander of the Air Force Tactical Air Command (where most of the Air Force fighter and attack aircraft resided), met with General Benny Peled, Israeli Air Force Commander, to establish a more professional relationship.[24] Dixon and Peled's ongoing discussions and the ongoing Air Staff analysis drove significant findings for the United States Air Force. Although the Israeli Air Force (IAF) suffered considerable damage in the war, they overcame enormous obstacles and prevailed in the conflict. After an initial examination and assessment of the Yom Kippur conflict, the United States Air Force focused on four operational areas identified as most impactful to its future success—air superiority, doctrine and training, logistics, and professional military education.

Although it may appear counter intuitive, the U.S. Air Force deemed air superiority essential in any future conflict even though ground-based systems inflicted the majority of IAF casualties. The accumulated IAF losses prompted the Air Force to redefine air superiority to focus on aircraft freedom of action throughout the entire combat theater.[25] Destroying Integrated Air Defense Systems (IADS) became a priority. Testifying before the Senate's Committee on Armed Services, Chairman of the Joint Chiefs of Staff, Admiral Moorer referenced the issue of air superiority and the Yom Kippur War. "Today, he said, gaining air superiority includes defeating SAMs in detail."[26] The Air Force recognized that suppression of these systems had to be viewed holistically, rather than as separate air campaigns. The Yom Kippur War review offered more insights into other systemic problems in the Air Force.

The second area of focus (Air Force tactics, doctrine, training, and organization) also arose from the postwar. Initially, the Air Force sought to understand why the Israeli air tactics and doctrine proved so inadequate during the early stages of the war. Many of the tactics and doctrine the Israelis had employed resembled those the U.S. Air Force would employ during a major conflict against the Soviet Union and the Warsaw Pact. Did a systemic problem exist in Air Force doctrine and training? The failure and ineffectiveness of these procedures required the Air Force to critically reexamine how to adjust in future conflicts. The conventional consensus of Air Force leadership and war planners held that superior air domain training enjoyed by the U.S. and NATO allies would overcome the Soviet and Warsaw Pact forces' numerical advantage. Quality over quantity was the mantra of American airmen yet, after the Yom Kippur War a new mantra appeared, "quantity has a quantitative advantage all its own."[27] Learning to fight and win while outnumbered was now a critical skill for the Air Force. U.S. airmen could no longer assume that quality in training and equipment would win the day. The focus on command-and-control platforms such as the Airborne Warning and Control System (AWACS) became a priority to the Air Force. This system would help overcome the numerical advantages of the Soviet and Warsaw Pact forces with enhanced intelligence and early warning advantages.[28]

The lessons learned from the Israeli Yom Kippur War experience in doctrine, organization, and tactics were not all based in previous poor performance. One important positive lesson for the U.S. Air Force regarded Israeli organizational tactics and doctrine in aircraft maintenance. The Air Force studied how the Israelis generated such high sortie rates despite significant combat losses. That study spurred changes in U.S. Air Force maintenance structures.

Lesson three concerned the high expenditures of munitions and other equipment during the conflict. Examining the materiel requirements for a high-intensity air campaign became essential for the USAF. The requirement to reinforce and resupply Israel during the war exposed organizational weakness in the United States Air Force's air mobility competency. The need for Mobility Airlift Command (the premier air transportation arm of U.S. government) to coordinate with other major United States Air Force commands to move supply and equipment proved problematic. The necessity for command unity in such an effort became readily apparent.

The fourth, and perhaps most important lesson for the Air Force from the Yom Kippur War, was the immediate need to shape its leaders' ability to think critically about future conflicts. Here it is important to reflect upon Eliot Cohen and John Gooch's *Military Misfortunes: The Anatomy of Failure in War*.[29] Cohen and Gooch, two world-class scholars in strategy and military history, outlined the importance of critical thinking to military leadership and combat success. Referencing Carl Von Clausewitz, the nineteenth-century Prussian military theorist, Cohen and Gooch championed studying the varied aspects of war, from the political down to the tactical, because all these levels will factor into the outcome of the conflict.[30] One of the major themes of the book was the importance of military organizational learning. Successful organizational learning was the key to gaining victory and the lack of such learning often spelled disaster for military forces. One of the World War II examples used in the book was the inability of the United States Navy to learn from the British Navy's experience of overcoming the German U-Boat threat. The U.S. Navy paid a fearsome price in blood and treasure before it was able to rectify the problem.[31] However, the United States Air Force was determined to learn from previous conflicts and find a way to use the Israeli experience in the Yom Kippur War.

How the United States Air Force would institutionally inculcate the consequential lessons gleaned from the conflict into the long-term thinking of the force would prove critical to its future success. As a result, the Air Force considered its Professional Military Education (PME) system and how it had developed past and current leaders, vis-à-vis how to shape its future leaders. How the Air Force examined these four major areas of concern after the Yom Kippur War will indicate more clearly whether the U.S. Air Force assumed the characteristics of Senge's learning organization to effect the needed changes.

SELF-EVALUATION

The Air Force approached the four focus areas systematically and conducted internal and external examinations of its processes and functions to find solutions to the issues they had identified. Its Tactical Air Command (TAC) (responsible for operations, doctrine, training, and readiness of all United States Air Force fighter and attack aircraft within the continental United States) assumed the overall responsibility to examine the first two focus areas, air superiority and changes in doctrine, tactics, and organization. TAC began a comprehensive review of how it would deal with the enormous array of Soviet Air Defenses systems that had devastated the Israeli Air Force. If war came to Central Europe by way of attacking Soviet forces, American airpower would be critical to gain aerial control. Without this air support, NATO forces could not blunt the Soviet Union and the Warsaw Pact major armored formations short of using tactical nuclear weapons.

Air superiority presented a multi-dimensional problem for the U.S. Air Force. In addition to the systematic analysis, the issue also required concrete changes to the Air Force business practices. Changes in training, tactics, and doctrinal approaches, the basis of the second Yom Kippur War focus item, had to be viewed through the lens of air superiority. Since the Air Force had established air superiority as a core mission, these changes required immediate action. Therefore, as one of the first initiatives following the Yom Kippur War, Tactical Air Command focused attention on understanding and fixing any issues regarding air superiority.

Regarding air superiority, the Air Force had already established a new training regimen requirement because of its less than desirable performance in the Vietnam War. The enemy-to-friendly kills ratio in aerial dogfighting did not rise to the level seen in the Korean War.[32] Yet, the Israeli experience in the Yom Kippur War, utilizing American frontline equipment, added weight to the argument to establish a new training program. The "Red Flag" training program at Nellis Air Force Base, Nevada, was developed to hone the skills of American airmen and close the performance gap. Although Red Flag was not strictly the result of the Yom Kippur War, it established the goal to simulate an intensive air combat training program in the first days of a conventional battle with the Soviet Union.[33] In this large-scale exercise, airmen from all different specialties participated in a vigorous wartime simulation. In addition to maximizing aircraft sortie generation for ground crews, the program included training aircrews on rescue, escape, and evasion techniques.[34] Although an expansive exercise, the major focus was devoted to fighter pilots who received the most realistic training, which required Red Flag participants to fly against U.S. Air Force aggressor squadrons trained to mimic tactics of Soviet and Warsaw Pact pilots in aerial engagements. Additionally, electronic equipment replicating Soviet air defense capabilities were placed on a sophisticated instrumented range complex to afford pilots the capacity to counteract those defenses. Participants also studied Soviet tactics in detail during these war games with particular attention paid to how the United States Air Force could overcome the Soviet force's numerical superiority.[35]

Because the exercise was designed to closely replicate aerial combat, the Air Force waived many of the normal safety restrictions, particularly involving low level flight, which resulted in a higher exercise-related accident rate. However, as pilots and aircrews recognized the rigor of the program, safety rates eventually rose to established Air Force standards.[36] The results of the Yom Kippur War gave American pilots an added incentive to sharpen their skills. It also prompted the Air Force to make other structural changes, as well.

The Red Flag exercises generated a more robust notion of air superiority and allowed pilots to hone their dogfighting skills. The exercises also incorporated enemy air defense suppression and electronic warfare attack against integrated air defense systems. The Air Force employed this multi-faceted aerial training to gain freedom of movement in the skies and enhance the prospect for victory by American forces.[37] TAC looked beyond the Red Flag exercises to other organizational, training, and doctrinal changes to improve the air forces' performance.

Organizationally, Tactical Air Command examined its maintenance structures and doctrine. Specifically, they calculated how they could increase their wartime fighter squadron productivity and maintenance effectiveness. The United States Air Force maintenance personnel stood in awe of the Israeli Air Force's (IAF) ability to generate air sorties during the intense combat of the Yom Kippur War.[38] A TAC maintenance team visited Israel after the war; they attributed the rapid turnaround of aircraft during the conflict to the IAF's new organizational structure. The Production Oriented Maintenance Organization (POMO) allowed the Israelis to quickly assess the viability of the aircraft to perform its next mission immediately after it landed. Maintenance, electronics, munitions, or airplane power plants specialists were embedded in one unit with the sole responsibility of regenerating aircraft to quickly rejoin the fight. This Aircraft Generation Squadron integrated cross-utilized specialists, which increased Israeli efficiencies.

The Israelis had formed two other squadrons under this maintenance concept (Component Repair and Equipment Repair Squadrons) to fix substantial maintenance problems and perform advanced repairs, which their aircraft generation squadrons could not accomplish individually. The U.S. Air Force initially adopted this new structure, but testing revealed that the expected operational and sortie generations rates did not increase.[39] Over longer periods of time, deferred maintenance problems eventually caused lower operational ready rates. Eventually, the Tactical Air Command modified the Production Oriented Maintenance Organization (POMO) structure to the Combat Oriented Maintenance Organization (COMO). This new structure further decentralized each squadron's maintenance activity to allow each unit to conduct their own scheduling and placed sortie utilization rates squarely on the squadron.[40] This structure afforded each squadron aircraft maintenance unit its own wing level maintenance and supply liaison and crew chiefs dedicated to each aircraft. The U.S. Air Force's ability to test its own capability and adapt and modify the IAF structure again proved their capacity to learn and adapt procedures and organizational structures to meet its own unique requirements.

Yet, advanced training and organizational changes alone would not overcome the daunting challenges the Soviet Integrated Air Defense System (IADS) posed. The Yom Kippur War review provided part of the impetus to discover additional means to gain air superiority. Without the ability to evade or neutralize a networked air defense system, casualties among American forces would be prohibitive. Tactical Air Command (TAC) then considered a materiel solution to overcome the formidable Soviet IADS challenge. In this case, TAC examined and exploited stealth technology to gain advantage over Soviet forces in any future conflict.

Three years after the Yom Kippur War, the U.S. Tactical Air Command initiated the stealth aircraft program with Skunk Works, a highly classified division in southern California that housed Lockheed Martin Corporation's most advanced aerospace development projects.[41] The U.S. Air Force determined that development of stealth aircraft capable of penetrating heavily defended areas undetected would prove a key factor in gaining air superiority. Although not designed as an air-to-air fighter, the stealth technology allowed USAF bombers to penetrate Soviet airspace undetected, drop precision ordinance, and destroy key command and control facilities, rendering them useless.

In *Skunk Works*, Ben Rich and Leo Janos, former heads of the stealth division, discussed how American industry and the U.S. Air Force developed the F-117 Nighthawk stealth fighter. Rich and Janos emphasized that lessons learned from the Yom Kippur War proved key to the development of this aircraft.[42] In a classified briefing to Lockheed Martin at the conclusion of the war, the Air Force suggested that if the loss rate of Israeli aircraft was extrapolated to a fight between the United States and Soviet Union on the European Central Front, the United States Air Force would run out of aircraft on day seventeen of the conflict.[43] The Israeli Air Force experience in the Yom Kippur War served as a wake-up call for all American airmen who could potentially face the Soviet air defenses in Europe. The United States Air Force could not hope to win a war of attrition in the skies of Central Europe. However, the advent of stealth technology would give American forces an advantage to compensate for Soviet air defenses—an advantage the IAF never had.

The USAF never viewed stealth technology as a panacea to the problem of air superiority. The limited number of aircraft produced (fifty-nine), and the cost and secrecy around the program, meant stealth capability enabled non-stealth aircraft to exploit holes in the air defense and communications networks they faced.[44] This capability proved devastatingly effective in January 1991 when the USAF launched F-117s against Saddam Hussein's Iraqi forces in Operation Desert Storm. Because these aircraft penetrated undetected deep into Iraq, the F-117s dropped precision bombs on Saddam's air defense headquarters, thus paralyzing Iraq's integrated air defense system. This action allowed hundreds of non-stealth aircraft to conduct effective bombing raids in Iraq. Training, doctrine, organizational updates, and materiel solutions continued to expand based upon the lessons of the Yom Kippur War. However, the relationship that would have the most profound effect on the United States Air Force's fighting concept was its new relationship with the United States Army.

The initiatives the Tactical Air Command employed to realize the air superiority that eluded Israeli air forces in the opening days of the war included a joint agreement to use Air Force and Army aviation and artillery assets to destroy Soviet Air Defense systems.[45] The partnership between Tactical Air Command and the United States Army's recently formed Training and Doctrine Command (TRADOC) comprised a main component of an external effort to innovate ways to avoid the issues the Israeli defense forces faced in the Yom Kippur War. The goal of the TAC-TRADOC partnership was to evaluate the policies, doctrine, and tactics to leverage cooperation on the battlefield to defeat Soviet and Warsaw Pact forces.

By the middle of the 1970s, the growing Soviet military capabilities incentivized both the Air Force and Army to find countermeasures.[46] Both services understood the importance a systematic approach to examine the Soviet military and develop a methodology to defeat their numerically superior forces. As a result, TAC and TRADOC developed a Joint Air-Land Forces Applications (ALFA) agency in 1975.[47] The agency's major commitment was to study joint methods to suppress enemy air defenses. Eventually this thinking was codified in Air Force doctrine. The 1992 edition of Air Force manual 1-1, *Basic Aerospace Doctrine of the United States Air Force*, states, "the Israeli attack across the Suez Canal [was cited] as an example of useful air ground synergy, in which land forces can be an especially effective mean for degrading the enemy's surface-based defenses."[48] In this case the doctrine specifically referred to the Israeli crossing of the Suez Canal and the destruction of the Egyptian Integrated Air Defense System (IADS), not by air forces, but by armored and infantry formations of the Israeli Defense Forces. The study of Israeli actions by the joint Army and Air Force applications group helped to cement the synergy of the Army–Air Force team in suppressing a Soviet Integrated Air Defense System (IADS). In addition, for the United States Army the destruction of Soviet air defense would afford U.S. air power a free hand in conducting Close Air Support (CAS) and Battlefield Air Interdiction (BAI).

How to refine and coordinate close air support and battlefield air interdiction became critical items for tactical review and inclusion into doctrine. CAS, the ability of aircraft to destroy targets on the ground in near proximity to friendly forces, was what the Israeli Air Force attempted to do in the early stages of its fight with the Egyptians and Syrians that proved so problematic. BAI is the ability to destroy or inhibit enemy forces preparing to move toward the forward edge of the battle zone to engage frontline forces. For the United States Air Force, the realm of BAI was directed at the second and third echelon of Soviet troops arrayed against U.S. and NATO forces in Central Europe. The emerging joint military doctrine postulated that, through BAI, the U.S. Air Force would significantly reduce the effectiveness of Soviet military formations. The attrition of the second and third Soviet echelons would ensure that the U.S. Army and NATO faced a reduced threat from additional waves of Soviet tanks and equipment.[49] As cooperation between the Air Force and the Army grew, the services signed two formal joint agreements. The first, a Memorandum of Understanding (MOU) signed on May 22, 1984, outlined thirty-one joint initiatives and "promised an unprecedented degree of inter-service cooperation."[50] The MOU outlined equipment and organizational requirements and addressed the joint tactics required to fight Soviet forces including logistic and airlift requirements to meet future battlefield needs.[51]

The agreement between the Army and the Air Force to support battlefield air interdiction provided distinct organizational benefits for the Air Force. The acquisition of new fighter and attack aircraft needed to accomplish that mission meant that the Army would not oppose defense budget spending for those items.[52] In the defense budget battles during the Cold War build up, having a service ally to support your acquisition priorities was critical. The Department of the Navy and other entities within the Department of Defense attempted to sway administration officials and legislators toward their own priorities. Yet, the partnership between the Air Force and the Army proved a formidable alliance for gaining equipment acquisitions.

The thirty-one initiatives MOU codified the relationship allowing both services to evaluate and coordinate air defense, close air support, and deep strike.[53] A second MOU, signed on July 11, 1984, specified that both the Air Force and the Army would "organize, train, and equip a compatible, complimentary, and affordable Total Force that will maximize our joint combat capability to execute airland combat operations."[54] These MOUs and the continued work with the Air Land Forces Application (ALFA) group were the biggest external operations the Air Force pursued based upon the lessons from the Yom Kippur and the perceived Soviet threat.

While ensuring the importance of air superiority and addressing tactics, doctrine, and organization, the Yom Kippur War also exposed other Air Force issues. The requirements for greater war stocks and the ability to transport vast amounts of men and materiel to support a large-scale war effort overseas comprised the third focus item that garnered the attention of the Air Force. The Air Force organizations that focused on these efforts were Military Airlift Command (MAC) and Air Force Logistics Command (AFLC).

The Air Force established the Military Airlift Command (MAC) in 1966 as the single Department of Defense agency operating airlift services.[55] MAC was in the best position to provide rapid resupply to the Israelis because it held the primary mission to provide strategic airlift for American military forces. President Nixon ordered MAC to begin resupplying Israeli forces. Thus began one of the most impressive displays of military air resupply ever witnessed. "From the arrival of the first mission on October 14 through the landing of the last aircraft at Lod Air Base in Israel on November 14, MAC's combined force of C-5s and C-141s airlifted 22,318 tons of material to Israel."[56] Operation Nickel Grass was largely credited for being a decisive factor in the ultimate Israeli tactical victory. Yet, others outside the Air Force uncovered flaws within the massive resupply efforts.

A report to the Congress of the United States by the General Accounting Office (GAO), an executive branch of the United States government, highlighted MAC airlift operations during the 1973 Yom Kippur War. Although initially hailed as a success and a demonstration of American logistical prowess, MAC officials noticed several flaws in their program. MAC leadership realized that these resupply shortcomings would be magnified significantly if called upon to resupply U.S. and NATO troops fighting in Central Europe. The GAO documented several problem areas to include: "inflight aircraft refueling capability, contingency plans for support of operations in the Middle East, improved management of airlift resources and the need to develop a capability to effectively command, control and communicate with its forces during a crisis."[57]

Required inflight refueling capability for airlift forces was crucial. During operation Nickel Grass, Military Airlift Command's inability to deliver equipment into Tel Aviv without interim stops in Europe for refueling proved problematic. The United States' NATO partners in Europe refused aircraft headed to Israel to land and refuel, and even refused overflight permission to military aircraft bound for Israel due to political situations.[58] An Arab oil boycott against Europe's tacit support of Israel gave the European nations pause when considering support for the American supply and equipment airlift. In 1973, the C-141 aircraft, which provided the bulk of MAC's intercontinental airlift, lacked air refueling capability.[59] Additionally, although the sixty-five C-5A aircraft provided MAC the ability to airlift oversized cargo (such as the Army's M-60 Main Battle Tank), and had aerial refueling capabilities incorporated in its design, none of its aircrews were qualified to perform such maneuvers.[60] This became challenging when European countries denied overflight or refueling stops. "Post-action studies by MAC also showed that aerial refueling could have reduced the number of airlift sorties by at least 100 and saved 48.5 million pounds of fuel."[61]

General Paul Kendall Carlton, the Commander of Military Airlift Command, who spearheaded the airlift of supplies to Israel, was justly proud of his command's accomplishments. However, he understood that major reforms were needed in strategic airlift for the United States. By January 1977, those efforts to rectify the shortcomings exposed during the Yom Kippur War were well underway. Military Airlift Command called for C-141 renovation to include refueling capabilities on all the aircraft. Through concerted efforts with the

Air Force and the Department of Defense General Carlton secured the contracts and funding to ensure the C-141 fleet upgrade. That upgrade included an extension to the body of the aircraft by 23.4 feet, allowing it to carry more cargo.[62] Carlton also mandated the immediate upgrade of seventy-seven C-5A aircrews to achieve certified mission capability for air-to-air refueling duties.[63] These adjustments now made the Military Airlift Command's fleet deployable worldwide without coordinating time-consuming en route refueling stops.

The command-and-control structures required to direct such a massive effort presented an additional issue for the U.S. Air Force strategic airlift. Many of the tactical or intra-theater Air Force airlift assets were distributed throughout the other Major Commands. Pacific Air Force (PACAF), United States Air Force Europe (USAFE), and Tactical Air Command all had assigned airlift assets. Having the visibility and control of all airlift assets would make the operation efficient. The lessons of the Yom Kippur War solidified the Air Force position that one single commander, with command and control over all air mobility assets, would provide a more efficient means of conducting business. Additionally, the strategic importance of a single military commander with the capacity to execute a worldwide airlift mission linked directly to the national command authority (President and Secretary of Defense) was highlighted during the Yom Kippur crisis. Only direct prodding by the President ensured that the various airlift components the United States Air Forces operated in Europe, Tactical Air Command, and Military Airlift Command responded to his request.[64] By the end of the decade the United States Air Force had reorganized and placed all airlift assets under Military Airlift Command control. Further, the Air Force had changed the designation of Military Airlift Command as a major command to a Specified Combatant Command, which would report directly to the National Command Authorities.

Air Force Logistics Command (AFLC) held organizational responsibility for providing worldwide logistics support to all the major entities in the Air Force. Air Force munitions fell directly under the purview of AFLC. The command had been instrumental in providing critical supplies and materiel for the Israeli Air Force during the Yom Kippur War. Four days after the start of the war, AFLC implemented a streamlined structure to support the Israeli government request for spares and munitions.[65] AFLC's ability to find and direct Air Force supplies and equipment to airbases where MAC and Israeli cargo aircraft could acquire and transport them to Israel directly supported the massive airlift MAC conducted. To ensure an easier process, AFLC decided to fill materiel requests directly from the Departments of State and Defense and then record the shortfalls from American stockpiles the fulfillment requests caused. These shortages were then reported directly to the

U.S. Air Staff at the Pentagon for future resolution.[66] The massive Israeli Air Force resupply consumed copious U.S. Air Force munitions and spares.[67] A top secret United States Institute for Defense Analysis report, conducted after the Yom Kippur War, revealed the U.S. Air Force was able to ship 3.53 short tons of air munition to Israel between October 15 and October 24, 1973.[68] That represented more than 15 percent of the air munitions stocks that the Israelis had on hand prior to the commencement of the war.[69] The heavy draw on American military supplies during the war revealed that the most acute shortage occurred with Air Force missile stocks. The United States Air Force Staff concluded that, for a future major combat engagement, "US Air Force holdings do not meet requirements, especially for air intercept and precision guided anti-radiation missiles."[70] For Air Logistics Command the necessity to provide streamlined War Reserve Materiel (WRM), contracting, and monitoring became critical relative to any future conflict. Finding new and better ways to rapidly replace the diminished inventories became an important initiative for AFLC. That effort continued to occupy the time and energy of AFLC for the next two decades.

As the United States Air Force worked systematically through the three focus areas identified after the Yom Kippur War (air superiority, doctrine and training, and logistics), the importance of professional military education became more acute. Professional Military Education (PME) comprises an important institution within the American military establishment. This institution helps convey the professional character of the United States military structure by highlighting service values and ideals to their students. In addition, and probably most importantly, PME provides an arena within which students can hone and sharpen intellectual talents. As a result, many of the military schools provide a master's degree in military art or strategic studies. Trevor Cutler outlined changes in Air Force Professional Military Education in the aftermath of the Yom Kippur War. He stated,

> [P]rofessional Military Education (PME) also received a new emphasis as the Air Force continued to reassess after the Yom Kippur War. PME served as an intellectual marketplace for new ideas as well as a reservoir of service culture and identity. Changes in institutions like the Air Force's Air University reflected those to the overall culture of the Air Force and how it viewed its future.[71]

In 1975, not long after the Yom Kippur War ended, Lieutenant General Raymond Furlong assumed command of Air University, the Air Force's headquarters that commanded all its professional military education for officer and enlisted personnel. General Furlong determined to place more emphasis on the study of air warfare versus national defense policy and decision making to ensure that the curriculum reflected this new priority.[72] Computer simulations and war gaming became essential parts of the new curriculum and the lessons from the Yom Kippur War were vital to the university's new operational focus.[73]

This new, more operationally focused professional military education system ensured that the lessons of the Yom Kippur War were incorporated into the thinking of its future leaders. A key lesson to emerge from the Yom Kippur War was the cost of underestimating your adversary. As a result, airmen participating in planning and combat simulations could no longer assume that previously successful tactics would work in the future. Additionally, the employment of precision guided air munitions and anti-tank weapons as essential tools in modern combat were considered. However, despite all the lessons devoted to operational tactics, hardware, and technology, the most important instruction for PME students concerned the importance of "imagination, daring, determination and superior execution," in military conflict.[74] Despite the Israeli force setbacks, particularly the Israeli Air Force, commanders found a way to overcome daunting challenges and reverse the initial gains of the Egyptian and Syrian forces. In modern war and society lessons Air Force professional military education students grappled with questions such as, "What was the impact of politics and technology in the 1973 Arab-Israeli War? How did the Egyptians use politics and technology to their advantage?"[75] Besides these broader strategic questions, students entertained questions that specifically focused on how the insights from the Yom Kippur War could relate directly to an American-Soviet conflict in Europe.[76] Finally, officers would have the opportunity to debate and vet the PME changes made in the force because of the conflict. The goal in exposing American military officers to these lessons was to ensure their ability to critically think through future challenges and avoid the turmoil that confronted the Israeli Air Force in the early stages of the Yom Kippur War.

The revised Air Force professional military education curriculum encouraged future leaders to form a shared vision of the institution's direction. The notion that airpower solely supported other elements of military power, such as the Army and Navy, was supplanted with the new idea that the Air Force, as an institution, could be strategic in its military effects.[77] This is not to say that the Air Force could win a war by itself, rather that the effects of airpower could change any enemy's strategic calculation. Air Force Colonel John Warden III, who would eventually become the Commandant of Air Command and Staff College, exemplified this new thinking about Airpower and expressed this in his book, *The Air Campaign: Planning for Combat* (1988). Warden, a career fighter pilot, used many examples from the Yom Kippur War in his book to advocate a new way to utilize airpower. He assessed that the Israelis paid a critical price early in the conflict by not gaining air superiority.[78] Gaining air superiority was foremost in any military campaign; however, once accomplished "the ability of airpower to achieve the strategic ends of war with maximum effectiveness and minimum cost" was significant.[79]

Warden analyzed the enemy as a system consisting of five concentric circles; leadership resided at the center, with organic essentials, infrastructure, population, and field forces occupying the remaining circles, respectively. Any air power campaign would seek to paralyze that system. Warden identified the leadership circle as the most important target, however, continuous attacks across critical nodes in any other circle would partially paralyze the entire system. This would give other military forces a distinct advantage.[80] Warden's theory was criticized given the Air Force's inability to dominate enemy forces in the Vietnam War. Warden would later amend his theory with the statement that "indeed, no nation enjoying air superiority has ever lost a war by the force of enemy arms."[81] His statement, however, failed to account for a lack of political will. Regardless, Colonel Warden's thinking about how to attack adversaries via air power proved critical in designing the air campaign against Saddam Hussein's Iraqi forces during Operation Desert Storm.

In concluding the examination of the United States Air Force's lessons learned from the Yom Kippur War, the organization's history clearly was a key factor in its ability to develop the disciplines required of a learning organization. Service leaders understood early that they had to harness new flight technology in a novel way. Learning to harness that technology correctly would eventually enhance America's military capability and defense. Continuous performance assessment after major conflicts was not new for the Air Force, yet the Israeli Air Force's high attrition rate during the Yom Kippur War and the USAF's own performance in the Vietnam War spurred a new dedication to learning and enhancing the performance of its force.

The Air Force utilized a comprehensive organizational approach to systematically study the effects of the Yom Kippur War and isolate transformative lessons. The site survey teams deployed to the battlefield soon after the war's conclusion as well as a new and open dialogue with senior Israeli Air Force leaders comprised part of the significant effort to gain experience-based information and learn new and better ways to combat future adversaries. Because the U.S. Air Force conducted an extensive performance examination in the aftermath of the Yom Kippur War (air superiority, new tactics and doctrine, logistics and command and control, and military education) the organization attained a clear and verified understanding of how to exploit the lessons of the Israeli experience.

New and innovative exercises such as Red Flag helped Air Force members individually hone and master their professional skills. Additionally, the Air Force employed mental models to conceptualize the Soviet Union's Integrated Air Defense threats and critically think through methods to defeat it. In partnership with the Army, the Air Force built shared vision via joint agreements to shape future battlefields utilizing the air land battle concept. Finally, the focus on professional military education enhanced team learning and elevated the dialogue between members of the profession, which increased service capabilities. Thus, the Air Force demonstrated all the characteristics of Senge's learning organization (systems thinking, organizational and personal mastery, the ability to question organizational models, and the benefit of a shared future vision).

Although not as methodical as the United States Army, the Air Force's history of constant change and adaptation of new flight technologies helped to position it as a learning organization. The Air Force clearly demonstrated the organizational effort to learn and adapt when they devastated Saddam Hussein's Iraqi forces during Operation Desert Storm starting in January of 1991. As discussed previously, the lessons Colonel John Warden gleaned from the Yom Kippur War proved instrumental in the design of the crippling air campaign conducted against an Iraqi armed force heavily equipped and organized by the Soviet Union. Its continuous efforts invested to transform itself into a potent and successful organization had proven successful in its Desert Storm campaign. It had indeed learned from the Yom Kippur War. Yet the lessons learned by the United States Air Force at the conclusion of the Yom Kippur War were far different than those the United States Navy incorporated into its organization. The next chapter will examine how the United States Navy learned from the Yom Kippur War.

NOTES

1. Robert F. Futrell, *Ideas, Concepts, and Doctrine: Basic Thinking in the United States Air Force 1907–1960* (Maxwell Air Force Base, AL: Air University Press, December 1989), 47.

2. Futrell, *Ideas, Concepts, and Doctrine*, 48.

3. The notion of strategic and tactical employment of aeronautics goes back to the earliest thinkers in U.S. Air Service. General Billy Mitchell defined the principal mission and secondary employment of aeronautics in a 1920 paper titled "Tactical Application of Military Aeronautics." In this paper Mitchell divided combat aviation into four categories, pursuit, bombardment, attack, and observation. These categories of aviation remained in the Air Force for many years. Pursuit aviation eventually was replaced the term fighter. See Futrell, *Ideas Concepts, Doctrine*, 33.

4. Carl H. Builder, *The Masks of War: American Military Styles in Strategy and Analysis* (Santa Monica, CA: Rand Corporation, 1989), 19.

5. Air Force Historical Support Division, "1949—The Berlin Airlift," https://www.afhistory.af.mil/FAQs/Fact-Sheets/Article/458961/the-berlin-airlift/, accessed February 10, 2019.

6. Robert F. Futrell, "Air Mission Accomplished," Readings Book 2 Military Strategy Analysis DS-611 (Maxwell Air Force Base, AL: Department of Aerospace Doctrine and Strategy-Air University), 186.

7. Futrell, "Air Mission Accomplished," 186.

8. Robert F. Futrell, "Air Mission Accomplished," in *The United States Air Force in Korea, 1950–1953* (Washington, DC: Office of Air Force History, 1983), 697.

9. Futrell, "Air Mission Accomplished," 697.

10. Futrell, "Air Mission Accomplished," 698.

11. Futrell, "Air Mission Accomplished," 693–697.

12. Robert F. Futrell, "The Strategic Bombing Campaign," in *The United States Air Force in Korea, 1950–1953* (Washington, DC: Office of Air Force History, 1983), 195.

13. Futrell, "The Strategic Bombing Campaign," 196.

14. For a comprehensive explanation of airpower theory and its legacy after the Vietnam War, see Mark Clodfelter, "The Limits of Airpower or the Limits of Strategy: The Air Wars in Vietnam and Their Legacies," *Joint Forces Quarterly* 78 (July 1, 2015), https://ndupress.ndu.edu/Publications/Article/607706/the-limits-of-airpower-or-the-limits-of-strategy-the-air-wars-in-vietnam-and-th/#:~:text=Airpower%20was%20a%20key%20%E2%80%9Cmeans,the%20air%20strategy%20they%20followed.&text=For%20President%20Lyndon%20Johnson%2C%20victory,%2C%20stable%2C%20noncommunist%20South%20Vietnam, accessed April 24, 2021.

15. United States Air Force, "Bombing as a Policy Tool in Vietnam: Effectiveness," in Book 2 *Military Strategy Analysis DS-611,* (Maxwell Air Force Base, AL: Department of Aerospace Doctrine and Strategy-Air University, 1988), 292.

16. National Archives Vietnam War U.S. Military Fatal Casualty Statistics, https://www.archives.gov/research/military/vietnam-war/casualty-statistics, accessed February 10, 2019.

17. Benjamin S. Lambeth, *The Transformation of American Air Power* (Ithaca, NY: Cornell University Press, 2000), 48–49.

18. Jim Wilson, "The SR-1 and the Yom Kippur War," *Barnstormers.com*, 77 (August 2009), https://eflyer.barnstormers.com/2009/077-eFLYER-FA02-SR71.html?path=eFLYER/2009/077-eFLYER-FA02-SR71.html, accessed February 24, 2020.

19. *Assessment of the Weapons and Tactics used in the October 1973 Middle East War*, Arlington, VA: Weapons Systems Evaluation Group, October 1974, https://www.cia.gov/library/readingroom/docs/LOC-HAK-480-3-1-4.pdf, 77.

20. Joseph Doyle, "The Yom Kippur War and the Shaping of the United States Air Force" (Maxwell Air Force Base, AL: School of Advanced Air and Space Studies, Air University, June 2016); Trevor Cutler, "From Independence to Interdependence: The U.S. Air Force and Airland Battle, 1973–1985" (thesis unpublished, University of Calgary, 2015).

21. Doyle, "The Yom Kippur War," 28.

22. Doyle, "The Yom Kippur War," 28–29.

23. Doyle, "The Yom Kippur War," 31.

24. Doyle, "The Yom Kippur War," 32.
25. Trevor Cutler, "From Independence to Interdependence: The U.S. Air Force and AirLand Battle, 1973–1985" (thesis unpublished, University of Calgary, 2015), 36.
26. Doyle, "The Yom Kippur War," 63.
27. Cutler, "From Independence to Interdependence," 35. [The author heard this mantra time and time again as an aircrew member on AWACS, as Director of Operations, and Commander of a Tactical Control System Unit in Germany during the heart of the Cold War.]
28. Doyle, "The Yom Kippur War," 57.
29. Eliot Cohen and John Gooch, *Military Misfortunes: The Anatomy of Failure in War* (New York: Vintage Books), 1991.
30. Cohen and Gooch, *Military Misfortunes*, 45.
31. Cohen and Gooch, *Military Misfortunes*, 94.
32. Cutler, "From Independence to Interdependence," 28–29.
33. Lambeth, *The Transformation of American Air Power,* 62.
34. The author participated in numerous Red Flag exercises and witnessed first-hand how ground and air crews were put through their paces.
35. Lambeth, *The Transformation of American Air Power*, 82.
36. Doyle, "The Yom Kippur War," 76.
37. The author participated in Red Flag exercises and Green Flag exercises while a member of Airborne Warning and Control Systems aircrew. Both exercises were conducted at Nellis AFB. A Green Flag exercise denotes a major focus on Electronic Warfare training.
38. James C. Rainey and Cindy Young, ed., "Maintenance Organization: A Historical Perspective," in *Old Lessons New Thoughts: Readings in Logistics, History and Technology 2006* (Maxwell AFB, Gunter Annex, AL: Air Force Logistics Management Agency, January 2006), 27.
39. Rainey and Young, *Old Lessons New Thoughts*, 28.
40. Rainey and Young, *Old Lessons New Thoughts*, 28.
41. Ben R. Rich and Leo Janos, *Skunk Works* (New York: Little, Brown and Company, 1994), 41.
42. Rich and Janos, *Skunk Works,* 17–18.
43. Rich and Janos, *Skunk Works,* 18.
44. Rich and Janos, *Skunk Works,* 105.
45. Lambeth, *The Transformation of American Air Power,* 85.
46. Cutler, "From Independence to Interdependence," 36.
47. Richard G. Davis, "The 31 Initiatives: A Study in Air Force-Army Cooperation" (Washington, DC: Office of Air Force History, 1987), 28.
48. Doyle, "The Yom Kippur War," 86.
49. Davis, "The 31 Initiatives," 30.
50. Richard I. Wolf, "Air Staff Historical Study, The United States Air Force: Basic Documents on Roles and Missions" (Washington, DC: Office of Air Force History, United States Air Force, 1987), 413.
51. Davis, "The 31 Initiatives," 92.

52. Phil Haun, "Peacetime Military Innovation through Interservice Cooperation: The Unique Case of the U.S. Air Force and Battlefield Air Interdiction," *Journal of Strategic Studies*, (2019): 12, DOI: 10.1080/014-2390.2018.1557053.

53. Davis, "The 31 Initiatives," 414.

54. Davis, "The 31 Initiatives," 415.

55. Draft of Report to the Congress of the United States: Airlift Operation of the Military Airlift Command During the 1973 Middle East War, October 10, 1974 logistics Readiness Center IRIS Number 01015859, Air Force History Index.Org.

56. Air Mobility Command Museum, "Operation Nickel Grass," https://amcmuseum.org/history/operation-nickel-grass/, accessed September 14, 2019.

57. United States General Accountability Office, "Airlift Operations of MAC During 1973 Middle East War," Report to the Congress of the United States (October 1, 1974), IRIS Public Record K144.054-2V, 46.

58. Adam Wambold, "Operation Nickel Grass: Turning Point of the Yom Kippur War" (October 8, 2018), https://www.nixonfoundation.org/2014/10/operation-nickel-grass-turning-point-yom-kippur-war/, accessed April 22, 2021.

59. Arnon Gutfeld and Clinton R. Zumbrunnen, "From Nickel Grass to Desert Storm: The Transformation of U.S. Intervention Capabilities in the Middle East," *Middle Eastern Studies* 49, no. 4 (July 12, 2013): 623–644, DOI:10.1080/00263206.2013.798312

60. Gutfeld and Zumbrunnen, "From Nickel Grass," 629.

61. Gutfeld and Zumbrunnen, "From Nickel Grass," 630.

62. Gutfeld and Zumbrunnen, "From Nickel Grass," 623–644

63. Gutfeld and Zumbrunnen, "From Nickel Grass," 629.

64. Zach Levey, "Anatomy of an Airlift: United States Military Assistance to Israel during the 1973 War," *Cold War History* 8, no. 4, October 17, 2008: 488, DOI: 10.1080/14682740802373552.

65. John C. Brownlee, "Air Bridge to Tel Aviv: The Role of the Air Force Logistics Command in the 1973 Yom Kippur War," *Air Force Journal of Logistics* XV, no. 1 (Winter 1991): 35.

66. Brownlee, "Air Bridge to Tel Aviv," 35.

67. Doyle, "The Yom Kippur War," 41.

68. Assessment of the Weapons and Tactics Used in the October 1973 Middle East War, Weapons Systems Evaluation Group Report 249 (October 1974), https://www.cia.gov/library/readingroom/docs/LOC-HAK-480-3-1-4.pdf, accessed February 7, 2020, 80.

69. Assessment of the Weapons and Tactics, 80.

70. Assessment of the Weapons and Tactics, 80.

71. Cutler, "From Independence to Interdependence," 21.

72. Cutler, "From Independence to Interdependence," 24.

73. Gregory C. Kennedy and Keith Neilson, ed., *Military Education: Past, Present and Future* (Westport, CT: Praeger Publishers, 2002).

74. David A. Tretler, "The Arab-Israeli Conflict: 1967–1979," in *Modern Warfare and Society: Volume II, Military Theory, History, Doctrine and Strategy* (Maxwell Air Force Base, AL: Air Command and Staff College, August 1988), 37–25.

75. United States Air Force—Air University. "Block VIII: Thinking About War Summary," in *Thinking About War: Military Theory, History, Doctrine and Strategy* (Maxwell Air Force Base, AL: Air Command and Staff College, August 1988), 116.

76. Tretler, "The Arab-Israeli Conflict: 1967–1979," 37–25.

77. Lambeth, *The Transformation of American Air Power,* 298.

78. Doyle, "The Yom Kippur War," 91.

79. David S. Fadok, "John Boyd and John Warden: Air Power's Quest for Strategic Paralysis" (Thesis, The School of Advanced Airpower Studies, June 1994), 30.

80. Fadok, "John Boyd and John Warden," 30.

81. David R. Mets, "The Air Campaign John Warden and the Classical Airpower Theorists," (Maxwell Air Force Base, AL: Air University Press, April 1999), 62.

Chapter 4

The United States Navy and Its Reaction to the Yom Kippur War

It is fitting to save discussion of the United States Navy's lessons learned from the Yom Kippur War to the last, for it appears that the Navy benefited least from its exposure to the conflict. The first indication of this is the lack of published literature on the influence of the war on the service, as opposed to the extensive references for the Air Force and the Army. The second indication is the lack of any apparent connection between changes in U.S. naval force structure, weapons systems, leadership, doctrine, or strategies that can be tied to the Yom Kippur experience. What makes this observation noteworthy is that it was the Navy, not the Air Force or the Army, that came closest to actual combat during the Yom Kippur War when the American Sixth Fleet faced off against the Soviet Fifth *Eskadra* (Operational Squadron) in the Eastern Mediterranean Sea. Why the United States Navy benefited so little from the aftermath of the Yom Kippur War will be the central inquiry of this chapter. However, before conducting a detailed examination of the U.S. Navy's involvement and reaction to the Yom Kippur War it is critical to understand its historical culture, and where it was organizationally, at the beginning of the Yom Kippur War.

Although the Marine Corps is considered a separate service, their actions in response to the Yom Kippur War will also be considered in this chapter. The Marine Corps does not enter "the defense planning arena as an independent institutional actor with a significant voice in the national approach to strategy and or military force planning."[1] The Secretary of the Navy is the arbitrator for funding and strategic planning priorities to the Secretary of Defense for all military naval forces, to include the United States Marine Corps.[2] In essence the Secretary of the Navy functions as the civilian control mechanism to ensure the Marine Corps meets its requirements to organize, train, and equip its forces for combat.

A BRIEF HISTORY OF THE UNITED STATES NAVY

Established by the Continental Congress on October 13, 1775, the United States Navy has a long and illustrious history and the most enduring national defense mission to the country. They and the United States Marine Corps, which was established on November 10, 1775, represent the military arm of the present-day Department of the Navy. The U.S. Constitution states in Article II, Section 8, Paragraph 13, that the Congress shall have the power "to provide and maintain a Navy."[3] For a nation separated by oceans from the European and Asian continents and its most formidable competitors, the U.S. Navy has always provided a buffer and ensured the free flow of commerce vital to the nation's well-being.

From its founding, the U.S. Navy has negotiated enormous organizational changes. Other than the United States Air Force, the Navy was the service most affected by technology. From wind-powered sailing ships, to coaled fuel steam power, to modern day gas turbine and nuclear power vessels, the Navy incorporated enormous technological advances within its force. Additionally, oftentimes grudgingly, the Navy changed its mindset regarding force structure and doctrine when incorporating these new technologies. There is no better example of this than the evolution of the Navy's main capital ship assets from battleships to aircraft carriers.

From the end of the nineteenth century to the early parts of the twentieth century the United States Navy championed the battleship as its major war fighting asset. Built to survive while providing maximum firepower against enemy surface ships and coastal fortifications, these vessels proved their worth as a form of strategic diplomacy and in actions during World War I.[4] However, after World War I, a demonstration of the effectiveness of new technologies changed the thinking about the role of the battleship.

Aviation's potential and its effect upon sea power did not immediately resonate with the leadership of the U.S. Navy. Although interested in the new technology, organizationally the leadership of naval aviation was not given the capacity to direct funding or personnel requirements for programs.[5] This weakened the potential growth of aviation within the Navy. However, that situation would begin to take a dramatic turn. On July 21, 1921, pilots of the U.S. Army Air Service, under the command of Brigadier General Billy Mitchell, bombed a decommissioned German World War I battleship, the *Ostefriesland*. The Department of the Navy and the Air Services arranged the bombing test, which afforded Mitchell the opportunity to prove to the Navy that airpower posed a significant threat to Navy capital assets.[6] Despite push back by senior leaders of the Navy on the efficacy of Mitchell's test, the importance of naval aviation was soon recognized. "Mitchell's actions—the demonstration bombing and sinking of the battleship *Ostfriesland*, and his public and congressional attacks on the Navy and War Department attitude toward airpower—had, if nothing else, spurred the Navy to strengthen its own air arm and move toward the building of aircraft carriers."[7] That action commenced with the commissioning of the first Naval aircraft carrier, the USS *Langley* in 1922.[8] By December 7, 1941, the United States Navy had seven aircraft carriers in its inventory. In fact, in the decade prior to World War II, the Navy had been better organized than the Army in addressing issues of aviation and airpower.[9] However, as an institution the Navy was still not convinced that the battleship should be replaced as its primary war-fighting asset.

After the Japanese attack on Pearl Harbor in December of 1941 by carrier-based aircraft, and the loss and damage of nineteen Navy ships, including eight battleships, the Navy began to reassess the role of the aircraft carrier. The performance of aircraft carriers during the Pacific Campaign and the vulnerability of other naval vessels to air attack convinced the leadership of the Navy of the centrality of this new weapons system. As a result, by the conclusion of World War II, aircraft carriers became the prime means of the U.S. Navy's power projection. From post–World War I to the conclusion of World War II, the Navy demonstrated a capacity for organizational learning, given its use of new knowledge and experience and the changes made in doctrine and procedures to accommodate this new form of naval warfare centered on the aircraft carrier.

After America's World War II victory, a new adversary appeared that threatened its international interests. The spread of worldwide communism and the growth of the Soviet Union required the Navy to focus on a new form of strategic competition, thus began a "Cold War" with a near peer competitor.[10] After the devastation suffered in World War II, the Soviet Union rapidly rebuilt its military power and gained territory in Eastern Europe and Asia, which posed a daunting challenge to American interests worldwide. Despite the recent evidence of the U.S. Navy's ability to project American power globally, the Soviet Union developed world-class maritime capability, second only to the United States. Their submarine force posed a direct threat to interdict reinforcement and resupply of American and NATO forces in Europe should hostilities commence.[11] Early in the Cold War competition, American naval forces were put to the test helping to resolve one of the most intractable problems between the United States and the Soviet Union ninety miles off the coast of the Florida Keyes.

The closest the United States ever came to a nuclear confrontation with the Soviet Union resulted from the Soviet deployment of missiles to Cuba,[12] a key ally of the Soviet Union. Having supported the revolutionary takeover of Fidel Castro and resisted an ill-fated CIA attempt to overthrow him, the

Soviet Union was determined to protect this key foothold in the Western Hemisphere. The Soviet Navy and merchant fleet transported military troops, materiel, and nuclear capable missiles to the island. Once an American U-2 spy plane overflight confirmed the presence of the missiles on October 15, 1962, President Kennedy's administration sought their removal from Cuba. To coerce the Soviet Union to withdraw its Medium Range Ballistic Missiles (MRBM) from Cuba, Kennedy instructed the Navy to institute a quarantine around the Island. This course of action would prevent the introduction of additional Soviet nuclear-armed MRBM's and halt any additional Soviet combat forces from entering Cuban ports. The Soviet weapons quarantine proved instrumental in successfully ending the Cuban Missile Crisis for the United States. The Navy proved that its carrier strike groups were a formidable weapon in the Cold War conflict with the Soviet Union by utilizing two large aircraft carriers as the centerpiece of the task force blockade.[13] "The president found U.S. naval forces valuable not only for deterring nuclear or conventional conflict, but for enabling him to manage a crisis without resorting to aggression."[14] This crisis and the larger strategic competition with the Soviet Union confirmed the Navy's organizational priorities. Unlike the Air Force and the Army who examined their Vietnam War experience and found the need for organizational change, the Navy viewed many of its upgrades and existing processes as successful.

Although the Navy took part in the Korean and Vietnam conflicts, they fulfilled an ancillary role to the major U.S. warfighting effort. Certainly, naval personnel fought bravely in both conflicts. In Korea and in Vietnam, naval aviators played an important role in the respective air campaigns. In the Vietnam War, U.S. naval riverine and special warfare groups were critical in interdicting North Vietnamese and Viet Cong supply routes. However, the major activities of the U.S. Navy remained focused on securing global trade and the sea lines of communications, as well as projecting American power when and where needed.

Although global power projection was its major focus, the Navy did learn some vital lessons from its Vietnam War aviation experience. In November 1968, the Navy conducted a review of the performance of its air-to-air missiles during the war. Named after the Navy Captain who directed and conducted the study, the Ault report determined that only one out of ten air-to-air missiles fired resulted in the kill of an enemy aircraft.[15] One of the report's key observations was "the realization of improved aircrew performance . . . through increased missile and target allowances, better range facilities, more realistic air combat maneuvering training."[16] The bottom line was that Navy pilots needed better training if they were to employ their weapons systems effectively. They believed these lessons would be helpful in any potential combat with the Soviet Union. The report recommended the establishment of an advanced fighter weapons training school, where pilots could learn critical lessons before combat.

The school, known as "Top Gun," was established in March 1969 at Miramar Naval Air Station in California—the predecessor to the Air Force's Red Flag program established at Nellis Air Force Base, Nevada. Eventually, both programs would focus on defeating Soviet and Warsaw Pact aircraft and weapons systems. Yet, for the Navy the requirements for what Peter Senge calls system-wide thinking did not yet exist. Personal mastery, though required by navy fighter pilots, was not exhibited throughout the rest of the fleet. Neither were the other elements of Senge's learning organization (mental models, building shared visions, and team learning) incorporated service wide because of the Vietnam experience. Because the Navy focused primarily on the Soviet Union, its limited direct exposure during the Yom Kippur War did not spur the same level of organizational change.

In 1970, the Soviet Union made a bold statement during OKEAN 70, a naval operation where two hundred Soviet ships "exercised simultaneously in the Atlantic, Pacific, and Indian oceans and the Mediterranean Sea."[17] It again reinforced the U.S. Navy's stance that the Soviet Navy had a global reach and that the United States Navy had to be prepared to confront them on the open seas around the world. There was no doubt that the incoming Chief of Naval Operations' major focus had to be the Soviet Union.

By the 1970s, Chief of Naval Operations Admiral Zumwalt had outlined four major areas of concern for the U.S. Navy in "Project Sixty." In September 1970, Zumwalt addressed all Navy flag officers and Marine Corps generals in a Project Sixty memo, which emphasized that naval capabilities would focus on assured second strike, control of sealines and areas, projection of power ashore, and overseas presence in peacetime.[18] The assured second-strike capability referenced the Submarine Launched Ballistic Missile (SLBM) capability that the Navy maintained for nuclear deterrence. The other capabilities focused on a major conventional war with the Soviet Union. On the eve of the Yom Kippur War the leaders of the American naval forces pursued a maritime strategy that relied upon keeping heavily armed carrier task forces forward deployed across the globe and having U.S. Marines embarked on amphibious vessels ready to respond to contingencies.[19]

One more key aspect exists to understand U.S. Navy culture and its strategic mindset prior to the outbreak of the Yom Kippur War. Of all the services, the United States Navy has always demonstrated an implicit independence from the other branches of the armed forces. This was particularly true before October of 1986 and the enactment of the Goldwater-Nichols legislation, which mandated that all military forces work in concert within the Department of Defense. In his description of a learning organization Peter Senge outlines the importance of systems integration across the other disciplines he touts in the *Fifth Discipline*. Yet, for the Navy, its process integration resided internally. As former Chairman of the Joint Chiefs of Staff General David Jones remarked, "The Department of the Navy is the most strategically independent of the services-it has its own army, [the U.S. Marine Corps], navy, and air force. It is the least dependent on others. It would prefer to be given a mission, retain complete control over all the assets, and be left alone."[20] Throughout its history the Navy has responded to change effectively, however, the lessons learned were primarily aimed at its own organization and the defense of the maritime domain, rather than operating in concert with the Army and the Air Force.

On the eve of the Yom Kippur War U.S. Naval forces, under the Command of the Sixth Fleet, deployed to Mediterranean Sea on routine patrol. That deployment included two aircraft carriers. At the start of the conflict the *Franklin Roosevelt* was docked in Spain, the USS *Independence* in Greece. The Sixth Fleet had a total of forty-eight vessels at their disposal. Opposing that deployment was the Soviet Union's Fifth Eskarda Squadron. This squadron comprised part of an ongoing Soviet presence in the Mediterranean Sea with a total of fifty-two available ships. However, the Eskarda Squadron lacked an aircraft carrier for naval air support. This placed a premium on the Soviet force in locating the American carriers and being able to inflict heavy damage if any hostilities broke out between the two navies. Yet, once the conflict between the Arabs and Israelis began, the Sixth Fleet's instructions was to monitor the situation and stay out of harm's way. A previous conflict between the Arabs and the Israelis in 1967 resulted in a disastrous outcome for the U.S. Navy.

During the 1967 Arab-Israeli conflict, labeled the "Six Day War," the Israeli Air Force and Navy attacked the USS *Liberty*, a U.S. Navy intelligence gathering ship, leaving thirty-four American sailors, Marines, and civilians dead and the ship severely damaged. Eventually, official U.S. and Israeli inquiries determined that the ship had been mistakenly attacked. Both the Israeli Air Force and Navy believed that they were attacking an Egyptian warship.[21] The U.S. Navy did not easily forget this incident. Although the *Liberty* was in international waters when it was hit, it was still close enough to the conflict to be mistaken as a combatant. Six years after the *Liberty* incident Admiral Daniel Murphy, Commander of the Sixth Fleet, was not about to have any of his ships mistakenly attacked by the war's combatants. The U.S. Joint Chiefs of Staff instructed Adm. Murphy to remain neutral in the conflict and not give either the Arabs, Israelis, or most importantly, the Soviet Union any cause for provocation to ensure that his forces remain safely outside the immediate battle area.[22] Having sailed from its anchorage in Greece the *Independence* battle group remained south of Crete for the duration of the conflict.[23] Yet as the conflict persisted, tensions continued to build between the Sixth Fleet and the Soviet Mediterranean squadron, Eskarda. The Americans and the Soviets had different clients in this conflict and neither side was prepared to let their client experience total defeat.

As U.S. policy makers realized that Israel would not achieve as quick a victory as it had in the 1967 war, they had to calculate a new support strategy for the Israelis. The Soviet Union had assumed a large military equipment resupply effort to Egypt and Syria, and Israel implored the United States to replace its dwindling war supplies. As a result, the Sixth Fleet commenced U.S. assistance in a massive Israeli resupply effort. For political reasons, many American allies would not allow direct support of munitions and weapons passing through their countries to Israel. This lengthened the supply lines and put strain on navigational support for aircraft transiting from Europe and the United States to Israel. Fortunately, the Sixth Fleet was able to arrange ship support across the Mediterranean to provide key navigational aids for aircraft en route to Israel.[24] The Sixth Fleet played another key role by supporting the resupply of number of A-4 Skyhawk aircraft that were a mainstay in the Israeli Air Force. As part of the American support efforts to Israel, volunteer U.S. Navy pilots shuttled American A-4s from active-duty Navy units to Israel. Many of the aircraft came from bases in the United States. These fighters were refueled by aircraft launched from carriers in the Mediterranean Sea, and landed on other carriers, before they made their way into Israel.[25]

As the war progressed, tensions rose between the Sixth Fleet and the Soviet Mediterranean Squadron. The Soviet Union reinforced its Mediterranean Squadron and by the end of October it had reached a total of ninety-six ships.[26] This force included nuclear-powered submarines and large number of surface-to-surface-missile-armed combatants.[27] Moscow was determined to signal to the United States that it had a larger, more competent, and potent naval force than the one the U.S. had confronted during the Cuban quarantine and began to shadow the U.S. carrier groups south of Crete.[28] The American fleet realized it would be extremely vulnerable to Soviet surface-to-surface missiles and kept its aircraft aloft as a hedge against any type of preemptive attack.

A key turning point in the war came when a cease fire, agreed to by Israel and its Arab adversaries, broke down and Israel advanced toward the Egyptian and Syrian capitals. The Soviet Union put its airborne forces on alert and threatened to intervene unilaterally to stop the Israelis. This caused the United States to place all its military forces on DEFCON III, one of its highest defense conditions. The Sixth Fleet was reinforced with another carrier strike group, bringing the total to three in the Mediterranean. The U.S. began to consolidate their position around Crete, to block any Soviet attempt to direct airborne divisions into the conflict zone. Fortunately, diplomatic maneuvering moderated this tension and armed conflict between Soviet and U.S. forces did not come to fruition. With its focus on monitoring Soviet forces and the resupply efforts, the United States Navy played little attention to the performance of the Israeli Navy during the conflict.

As previously discussed in chapter 1, the Israeli Navy delivered the country's most important early success in the war. The Israeli Navy had decided in the mid-1960s to focus it naval power around armed missile boats.[29] This was, in no small part, based on the sinking of the Israeli Destroyer *Eilat* by an Egyptian Komar-class missile boat on October 21, 1967.[30] The Egyptian ship fired Soviet-made SS-N-2 Styx ship-to-ship missiles at the Israeli destroyer, which resulted in the death of forty-seven Israeli sailors with many more wounded.[31] This incident, and the lessons learned from previous conflicts, prompted the Israeli Navy to reassess their core missions. They determined that they had three major responsibilities to the Israeli Defense Force (IDF). The Israeli Navy's primary mission was to defend their coast from armed attack, second, eliminate any threat from Arab missile boats, and finally provide support to ground troops.[32] Based on those mission requirements, the Israelis selected a German boat design which, due to political considerations, they had manufactured in France. They designated the ship as the Sa'ar (Storm)-class missile boat. The Sa'ar ships were equipped with deck guns and Gabriel anti-ship missiles. The boats were fast and had small radar cross sections, which made it more difficult for their adversaries to locate them with radar and target them. In addition, the Israelis packed these new ships with electronic warfare gear that made it difficult for enemy ships to detect them, but if targeted they had the capability to jam or deceive incoming missiles.[33]

On the first night of the Yom Kippur War Israeli Sa'ar boats sank five Syrian naval vessels without losing any of their ships.[34] Two days later, off the Sinai coast, another squadron of Sa'ar missile craft sank two Egyptian missile patrol boats. The use of ship-to-ship missiles by the Israeli Navy was impressive. Although the Syrians and Egyptians were equipped with Soviet-made OSA missiles, which had a longer range than the Israeli Gabriel missiles, the Israeli Navy's skillful use of countermeasures and electronic warfare was ultimately successful. Yet, because these engagements took place in the littoral region, these events did not garner much attention from the U.S. Navy.

When the Yom Kippur War concluded, the Navy participated in several survey teams to assess the war's impact. Soon after the war, two Navy Captains visited Israel as part of the U.S. Military Operational Survey Team (USMOST). The Center for Naval Analysis produced a report in May 1974 on the Interaction of Arab/Israeli Naval Forces during the Yom Kippur War. Additionally, after a meeting with the Israeli Navy, an assessment was made of anti-ship missile defense systems capabilities as employed in the war.[35] These interactions were important, but they did not focus the attention of the U.S. Navy as did the interactions between the Israeli and the United States armies.

Finally, as part of the United States Military Equipment Validation Team-Israel (USMEVTI), U.S. Naval officers did examine the conflict zone, but they focused on the performance of the A-4 Skyhawk aircraft, not the performance of the Israeli Navy.[36] When Israeli A-4s flew at low level during the war to avoid Egyptian and Syrian medium altitude surface-to-air missiles (SAMs), they exposed themselves to enemy anti-aircraft guns and Soviet-made infrared guided Strela-2 man portable air defense systems. These weapons took a fearsome toll on the Israeli Air Force. They lost forty-nine Skyhawks during the war.[37] Yet overall, there was not a systematic examination and incorporation of lessons learned from the conflict as there was in the Air Force and in the Army. There was no shared vision that Senge discusses in the *Fifth Discipline* by the Department of the Navy. However, for the United States Marine Corps there were several lessons that they pulled away from the conflict that affected their organization.

THE MARINE CORPS

The Marine Corps has always had a symbiotic relationship with the Navy. Upon its founding on November 10, 1775, they were specifically designated for "service as landing forces with the fleet."[38] Throughout its history, the Marine Corps has provided a force in readiness to project power from the sea and to protect American naval installations around the globe. Other than World War I, when the Marines augmented Army ground forces in the trenches of Western Europe, the Marine Corps had been tied to its traditional role as an amphibious force in readiness, organized to project power globally. The caveat to this characterization of the Marine Corps was its extensive use in policing actions as part of American foreign policy, particularly in the Americas and the Caribbean between World War I and World War II. However, its core mission to project power from the sea remained its most potent capability. The most impressive demonstration of that capability was the Island-hopping campaign it conducted in the Pacific during World War II. In bloody conflicts throughout the Pacific, U.S. Marines seized territory to provide an unassailable line of communication from which American forces could attack Japan.

The Marine Corps learned vital lessons from that conflict. The most important was the need to have its own organic aviation elements to support its ground forces. The invasion of Guadalcanal was a pivotal event in that learning process. During that island invasion three naval aircraft carriers were tasked to support the Marine landing force. Later, due to a threat from

Japanese naval forces, the three carriers withdrew, leaving the Marine landing force without close air support.[39] For eleven days the Marines battled Japanese forces without close air support until Marine aviation aircraft landed at Henderson airfield in Guadalcanal. As an organization the Marines were determined never to be left without air support for their ground forces. During the conflict, the Marine Corps began the fledgling adaption of what would be known as the Marine Air and Ground Task Force (MAGTF). This organizational structure, which was codified in a Marine Corps order in 1963, would ensure that all elements of ground, aviation, logistic, and command and control would be under the purview of one unified Marine commander.[40]

Over the next years, the Marine Corps perfected their close air support execution in conflict zones. Ground force support became Marine Aviation's primary mission. All Marine aviators go through an officer basic course in which they learn how to perform as infantry first. The thought process for the Marines is that even as an aviator you will better understand the pressures and the difficulties of the infantrymen that you support if you first walk in their shoes. As one former Marine historian stated, "it's a matter of learning what an airplane can do to help ground troops accomplish their missions."[41] During the Korean and Vietnam conflicts Marine aviation supported its ground forces with close air support in addition to contributing to the overall air campaign. However, its major effort in each conflict was to contribute to the ground commander's effort in the theater.

In the Korean War, the Marines displayed their expertise in planning and executing a decisive, surprise amphibious landing at Incheon. Operation Chromite, the plan to seize Incheon, was critical to the Commander of American forces' efforts to reverse the North Korean attack.[42] As part of the U.S. Army's X Corps, the 1st Marine Division successfully landed at Incheon. In conjunction with U.S. Army forces, they seized the town of Incheon and retook the capital city of Seoul. Yet, after the August 1950 landing, the Marine Corps remained part of the ground campaign in Korea for almost three years, which took its toll on the service. As part of that ground campaign the Marines advanced into North Korea toward the Chinese border, near the Chosin Reservoir. Due to the overwhelming intervention of Chinese forces, the 1st Marine Division eventually retreated from the Chosin Reservoir. Although the Marines conducted the retreat in a courageous and orderly fashion the operation placed considerable strain on the force. A little more than a decade after fighting ceased in the Korean War, the Marines found themselves again enmeshed in a ground war in Asia. The Vietnam conflict would prove more onerous to the organization than its involvement in the Korean conflict.

After its initial February 1965 landing in Da Nang, Vietnam, the Marine Corps found itself fighting another long and drawn-out land campaign, replicating the U.S. Army experience in the war. When the conflict ended, nearly 500,00 Marines had served in Southeast Asia; close to 13,000 were killed in action and 52,000 wounded.[43] The outcome of the Vietnam War demonstrated the Marine Corps' need to reset as an organization. As the Marine Commandant said at the time, "We are pulling our heads out of the jungle and getting back into the amphibious business. . . . We are redirecting our attention seaward and reemphasizing our partnership with the Navy."[44] In much the same way, the aftermath of the Yom Kippur War provided the Marines the opportunity to think about how it would fight in a high-intensity conflict against mechanized and heavily armored Soviet and Warsaw Pact forces. Rethinking how they would be able to meet and defeat such forces in the littoral area in Northern or Southern Europe was a daunting challenge.

For the Marine Corps, the study of the Yom Kippur War also posed an institutional threat. The revelation of the effectiveness of precision-guided weapons (PGMs) such as ship-to-ship missiles, the air defense, and anti-tank weapons, placed considerable doubt on the efficacy of conducting an opposed amphibious landing in the future. One article by Marine Colonel C. V. Hendricks in the *Marine Corps Gazette* highlighted this factor stating, "absent a landing craft capable of matching the speed and range of a helicopter-borne force, PGMs in forcing amphibious shipping over the horizon, effectively neutralized much of the MAGTF's striking power."[45] Part of that MAGTF striking force required new amphibious helicopters and landing ships, yet the Marine Corps struggled with the Department of the Navy, its parent organization, to acquire new ships that would support a landing force in a high-intensity conflict. The problem for the Navy was that these new amphibious ships would compete with other ship-building priorities and modernization needed to compete with the Soviets in the open ocean.

The Yom Kippur War highlighted that matching Marine amphibious forces against Soviet armored and mechanized formations would be a difficult task, yet the Marines also learned some positive lessons in the conflict both from the Egyptian and Israelis forces.[46] First, the Marines took lessons from the Egyptian soldiers who demonstrated how proper training with the right weapon systems could enable infantry to inflict tremendous damage on armored formations. Meeting Soviet armor on the battlefield, "Marines armed with the right missiles could significantly even the odds."[47] Secondly, like their Army counterparts, the Marines were impressed by the Israeli soldiers' outstanding training. Their individual soldier skills and their flexibility allowed them to be resilient after the initial attacks from the Egyptian and Syrian armed forces. The Marines prided themselves on their own training, especially its Marine Air Ground Task Force (MAGTF) which integrated air, ground, logistics, and command and control elements under one formation. Finally, as part of that integrated air ground task force the Marines recognized the similarity in their air defense systems and command and control with the Israelis air defense forces.

The IDF and the Marines operated Hawk anti-aircraft missile batteries and similar long-range search radars. The low-level attack penetration of Egyptian and Syrian aircraft into Israeli forces indicated a gap in warning and detection. The Marines understood the importance of linking with Navy E-2C Airborne early warning aircraft, or linking with the larger, more capable United States Air Force E-3A Airborne Warning and Control System (AWACS) to detect low-level attacking aircraft.[48] All of these were mission critical priorities for the Marines. However, organizational viability was the biggest priority for the Marine Corps. If their amphibious capability and relevance were questionable in a major conflict with the Soviet Union and the Warsaw Pact, it would be essential that they demonstrate other vital defense capabilities.

After the Yom Kippur War the Marines again championed themselves as a ready-made combined arms team, capable of operating in uncertain times. Because they were forward deployed on ships that could respond rapidly to any contingency, the U.S. Marine Corps believed they offered defense planners flexibility. For larger, high-intensity conflicts, as contemplated with the Soviet Union and the Warsaw Pact, the Marines believed that their mere presence offshore could tie down Soviet and Warsaw divisions that might have to respond to an amphibious assault.[49] This thinking proved prophetic in 1991 as the Marines tied down Iraqi divisions during Operation Desert Storm, because they feared a potential amphibious assault.[50] However, in support of the overall ground campaign of U.S. forces dominated by the Army's AirLand Battle concept, the major assault of the Marines during Operation Desert Storm came not from the sea, but from their positions in Saudi Arabia.

SENGE AND THE NAVY AS A LEARNING ORGANIZATION

Placed against Peter Senge's criteria for highlighting learning organizations, the Department of the Navy proved far less amenable to using the experiences of the Yom Kippur War for its future learning. Israeli diplomatic and military historian David Rodman may have had the best insight as to the reason why the U.S. Navy seemed resistant to organizational learning from the Yom Kippur War. He reviewed the Central Intelligence Agency's assessment of the American views on the war and came away with a definitive assessment. In a telling paragraph, he writes:

About one quarter of the substantive portion of the CIA Report, or about twenty-five pages of text, is devoted exclusively to air warfare, whilst less than two pages of text is dedicated to naval warfare. The reason for this disparity is not hard to fathom. The clash between the IAF (Israeli Air Force) and Arab air defenses involved precisely the same doctrine, tactics and technology as those employed by contemporary NATO and WP (Warsaw Pact) armies. Thus, a thorough review and assessment of this aspect of the war would be useful in drawing lessons that could then be applied to the NATO-WP aerial balance of power. The clash between Israeli and Arab fast missile boats, on the other hand, was not pertinent to a NATO-WP confrontation at sea, which would be dominated by aircraft carrier groups and submarines, not small ships launching short-range missiles at each other.[51]

Indeed, as already chronicled in this chapter, the Chief of Naval Operations (CNO) at the time of the Yom Kippur War, Admiral Elmo Zumwalt, had given prior direction to the Navy on how they were to view their future competition with the Soviet Navy. In addition, Zumwalt was already completely engaged in bureaucratic infighting within the Navy trying to survive his tenure as CNO. A junior selection to the CNO post, Zumwalt incurred the wrath of other serving and retired senior naval leaders because of his innovative leadership style, including Z-Grams (a kind of pre-Twitter means of very quick and direct communications) that quickly communicated his ideas and feelings on naval matters to the fleet. These types of communications went against the Navy's rigid, formal chain of command structure in place for over a hundred years. As Carl Builder stated in the *Mask of War*, "the navy, much more than any of the other services has cherished and clung to tradition."[52] Zumwalt's efforts struck at the very heart of that tradition. His tolerance of informality, including longer hair styles and beards, riled the Navy traditionalists. Perhaps most annoying of all to senior leaders was Zumwalt's vision of a "High-Low" fleet mix that deemphasized the large nuclear-powered aircraft carrier as the centerpiece for the fleet and emphasized small and more numerous medium-to-small naval combatants.[53]

Yet for all his innovation there is room to criticize Admiral Zumwalt's approach based on Senge's organizational model. There is some indication that Zumwalt did see the naval problems of his time in systemic terms, but not much evidence that the institution of the Navy shared such a perspective. Thus, a systems view, especially one built from the experiences learned from the Yom Kippur War could have proved helpful for the Navy. For personal mastery, even in current times the Navy has sacrificed formal learning for on-the-job, that is fleet-at-sea, learning. There are certainly pros and cons to both methods of training, yet the standardization and quality control structure enhances personal mastery. The development of the "Top Gun School" to formally improve the performance of its fighter pilots was one instance when the Navy demonstrated a desire to train a segment of its force in personal mastery, but this was not spurred by the Yom Kippur War, nor was similar training in different specialties replicated across the Navy.

Again, the infighting within the Navy, especially under Adm. Zumwalt, allowed no shared vision. Additionally, except for Zumwalt and his staff, the institution failed to question the service's core mental models, as opposed to U.S. Army General Starry, as Commander of Army Training and Doctrine Command (TRADOC), who discussed trying to include the Navy in his AirLand Battle doctrine. Again, AirLand Battle was the mental model that the Army promulgated, however, this inclusive vision proved unsuccessful. Starry stated, "I had spoken to the Chief of Naval Operations a couple of times, several times as a matter of fact, about it and he knew what we were doing, but as far as the details were concerned, the Navy was not part of the dialogue."[54] The Navy's disinterest was indicative of their insular operations.

Finally, the team learning evidenced through Zumwalt's enforced training reforms did not survive past his tenure. Zumwalt, to his great credit, allowed Admiral Stansfield Turner, his newly appointed President of the Naval War College, to make dramatic changes in the Navy's premier learning institution. Called the "Turner Revolution," the President of the Naval War College advanced more scholarship and rigor into the War College experience. Turner developed the Naval War College into a first-class educational institution by hiring more PhD-level faculty and expanding students' intellectual exposure to renowned scholars and policymakers.[55] Yet, although the Navy had outstanding learning institutions in the Naval War College and its scientific and research university, the Naval Postgraduate School, it did not appear to tie performance at these institutions to assignments, nor did it tie advancement to success at any of these schools.[56] Again, General Don Starry commented that "the Navy has never put that kind of emphasis on progressive schooling that the other services have."[57] Additionally, he remarked, they have sent officers to school between assignments and did not use their school as a merit reward for their top performing officers.[58] One can concluded that the Navy was, and is, structurally oriented to learn from experience, but not processual in its application of those lessons. Again, from Senge's model of systems thinking, personal mastery, mental model, building shared vision, and team learning, the Navy did not use all these tools to progress from its observation and experience in the Yom Kippur War.

In conclusion, the Navy emerged from the wake of the Yom Kippur War convinced that its method of operations was sound for where it intended to conduct its work—the North Atlantic and Pacific Oceans. One can state that the Navy did not feel it necessary to learn or apply naval lessons from the Yom Kippur War, as the lessons seemed to apply to the littoral maritime domain, one that was not of primary concern to the Navy. However, when the Cold War ended sixteen years later, the Navy did begin to pay attention to littoral waters, the places where the Israeli Navy successfully battled the Arab navies. At the time of this writing the U.S. Navy has focused more attention on operating in the littorals of the Persian Gulf and the South China Sea.[59] However, it is unknown whether it will use the lessons of the Yom Kippur War to inform any changes in doctrine or capability.

NOTES

1. Carl H. Builder, *The Masks of War: American Military Styles in Strategy and Analysis* (Baltimore, MD: John Hopkins Press, 1989).

2. Irv Blickstein et al., *Navy Planning Programing, Budgeting and Execution: A Reference Guide for Senior Leaders, Managers, and Action Officers* (Santa Monica: Rand Corporation, 2016), 18.

3. The Constitution of the United States of America (Article I, Section 8, Paragraph 12) states that the Congress is given the power "to raise and support Armies, but no Appropriation of Money to that Use shall be for a longer Term than two Years." Paragraph 13 of the Constitution is often used by the Navy to highlight and differentiate the enduring nature of its mission and the requirement to provide and maintain their service without the necessity to raise funds in its own support.

4. The "Great White Fleet" was a prime example of using American battleships for strategic diplomacy. In 1907 President Teddy Roosevelt sent a fleet of sixteen U.S. battleships on a two-year global tour to demonstrate American naval power and reach. The hulls of these ships were painted white but their mere presence at ports around the world sent a clear message of American power.

5. Roy A. Grossnick, *United States Naval Aviation, 1910–1995* (Washington, DC: Naval Historical Center, 1997), 47.

6. John T. Correll, "Billy Mitchell and the Battleships," *Air Force Magazine* (June 1, 2008), https://www.airforcemag.com/article/0608mitchell/ accessed February 27, 2021.

7. Dewitt S. Copp, *A Few Great Captains: The Men and Events that Shaped the Development of U.S. Air Power* (McLean, VA: EPM Publications, 1980), 33.

8. Correll, "Billy and the Battleships."

9. Copp, *A Few Great Captains*, 33.

10. Builder, *The Masks of War*, 83.

11. John Hattendorf, ed., *US Naval Strategy in the 1970s* (Newport, RI: Naval War College Press, 2007), 11.

12. Curtis Utz, "The Cordon of Steel: The U.S. Navy and the Cuban Missile Crisis," *Naval Historical Center* (Washington, DC: Department of the Navy, 1993), 1.

13. Utz, "The Cordon of Steel," 22.

14. Utz, "The Cordon of Steel," 47.

15. "Report of the Air-to-Air Missile System Capability," review, *Naval Air System*, Department of the Navy, Washington, DC, January 1, 1969.

16. "Report of the Air-to-Air Missile System Capability," review, 21.
17. Hattendorf, ed., *US Naval Strategy in the 1970s*, ix.
18. Hattendorf, ed., *US Naval Strategy*, 4.
19. Hattendorf, ed., *US Naval Strategy*, ix.
20. Builder, *The Masks of War,* 31.
21. A. Jay Cristol, *The Liberty Incident: The 1967 Israeli Attack on the U.S. Navy Spy Ship* (Washington, DC: Brassey's Inc., 2002), 199.
22. Abraham Rabinovich, "The Little-Known US-Soviet Confrontation During the Yom Kippur War," *Global Post*, October 26, 2012, https://www.pri.org/stories/2012-10-26/little-known-us-soviet-confrontation-during-yom-kippur-war, accessed March 6, 2021.
23. Robert Weinland, "Superpower Naval Diplomacy in the October 1973 Arab-Israeli War" (Arlington, VA: Center for Naval Analyses, June 1978), 37.
24. Weinland, "Superpower Naval Diplomacy," 38.
25. Weinland, "Superpower Naval Diplomacy," 35.
26. Weinland, "Superpower Naval Diplomacy," 44.
27. Weinland, "Superpower Naval Diplomacy," 46.
28. Lyle J. Goldstein and Yuri M. Zhukov, *A Tale of Two Fleets: A Russian Perspective on the 1973 Naval Standoff in the Mediterranean* (BiblioGov, November 21, 2012), 46.
29. Sam Helfont, "Cultural Challenges for Israeli Sea Power in the Eastern Mediterranean," *Naval War College Review*, no. 1 (Winter 2021): 74.
30. "Central Intelligence Agency," Intelligence Report: The 1973 Arab-Israeli War: Overview and Analysis of the Conflict" (September 1975): 112.
31. Dove Zakheim, "The United States Navy and Israeli Navy: Background, Current Issues, Scenarios, and Prospects" (Arlington County, VA: Center of Naval Analysis [CNA], 2012), 4
32. Christian Heller, "The Impact of Insignificance: Naval Developments from the Yom Kippur War," *Center for Maritime Security,* (February 19, 2019).
33. Zakheim, "The United States Navy and Israeli Navy," 5.
34. Heller, "The Impact of Insignificance," 6.
35. *Assessment of the Weapons and Tactics Used in the October 1973 Middle East War* (Arlington, VA: Weapons Systems Evaluation Group, October 1974).
36. Joseph Doyle, "The Yom Kippur War and the Shaping of the United States Air Force" (Maxwell Air Force Base, AL: School of Advanced Air and Space Studies, Air University, June 2016), 21.
37. S. K. Au-Yeong, "The Mighty A-4 Skyhawk Was the U.S. Navy's Best Little Bomber," *The National Interest* (October 27, 2015).
38. "Brief History of the United States Marine Corps," Reference Branch USMC History Division (July 2006), https://www.usmcu.edu/Research/Marine-Corps-History-Division/Brief-Histories/Brief-History-of-the-United-States-Marine-Corps/ accessed March 8, 2021.
39. Richard Rasmussen, "Marine Corps Close Air Support Development From Guadalcanal to Okinawa" (Master of Military Studies Research Paper, Marine Corps

Command and Staff, April 2011), https://apps.dtic.mil/dtic/tr/fulltext/u2/a600543.pdf, accessed March 8, 2021.

40. "What Is a MAGTF?," United State Marine Corps Official Website (2021), https://www.26thmeu.marines.mil/About/MAGTF/#:~:text=The%20MAGTF%20 was%20formalized%20by,It%20stated%3A&text=Since%20World%20War%20 II%20in,sufficient%20sustainability%20for%20prolonged%20operations, accessed March 13, 2021.

41. "100 Years of Marine Aviation," *Air and Space Magazine* (March 12, 2012), https://www.airspacemag.com/military-aviation/100-years-of-marine-aviation-20911884/, accessed March 8, 2021.

42. Lynn Montross and Nicholas Canzona, *U.S. Marine Operations in Korea 1950–1953, Volume II, The Inchon-Seoul Operation* (Historical Branch, G-3 Headquarters U.S. Marine Corps, Washington, DC, 1955), 62.

43. "U.S. Marines in Vietnam: 1954–1975," Marine Corps University, https://www.usmcu.edu/Research/Marine-Corps-History-Division/Brief-Histories/Marines-in-Vietnam-1954-1975/ accessed on March 8, 2021.

44. Ian T. Brown, *A New Conception of War*: *John Boyd, the U.S. Marines, and Maneuver Warfare* (Quantico, VA: Marine Corps University Press, 2018), 43.

45. Brown, *A New Conception of War*, 50.

46. Brown, *A New Conception of War*, 48–49.

47. Brown, *A New Conception of War*, 54.

48. Martin Musella, "Air Operations During the 1973 Arab-Israeli War and the Implications for Marine Aviation," Marine Command and Staff College (April 1, 1985), https://www.globalsecurity.org/military/library/report/1985/MML.htm, accessed March 9, 2021.

49. Brown, *A New Conception of War*, 52.

50. Ronald Brown, *U.S. Marines in the Persian Gulf, 1990–1991 with Marine Forces Afloat in Desert Shield and Desert Storm* (Washington, DC: History and Museums Division Headquarters, U.S. Marine Corps, 1998), 133.

51. David Rodman, "Eagle's-eye View: An American Assessment of the 1973 Yom Kippur War," *Intelligence and National Security* 31, no. 4 (March 5, 2015): 507.

52. Builder, *The Masks of War,* 18.

53. Elmo R. Zumwalt, Jr., *On Watch: A Memoir* (New York: Quadrangle/New York Times Books, 1976). Chapter 4 discusses the High-Low Fleet mix concept in detail.

54. Sorley, *Press On!* 2, 1274.

55. John B. Hattendorf, Jr., et al., *Sailors and Scholars: The Centennial History of the U.S. Naval War College* (Annapolis, MD: Naval Institute Press, 1984) discusses the Turner Revolution in detail. In sum, this academic revolution was a comprehensive curriculum reform coupled with a faculty requirement for more academic credentials.

56. An insightful look into the long history of U.S. Navy lack of concern for professional education can be found in a USNI blog article by Will Beasley, "The Rise and Fall of U.S. Naval Professionalism," February 2015, at https://blog.usni.org/2015/02/06/the-rise-and-fall-of-u-s-naval-professionalism, accessed February 13, 2017.

57. Sorley, *Press On!* 2, 1035.
58. Sorley, *Press On!* 2, 1240.
59. "Advantage at Sea: Prevailing with Integrated All-Domain Naval Power," Department of the Navy, Washington, DC (December 2020): 25.

Chapter 5

Analysis and Conclusion

This book set out to examine the effect the 1973 Yom Kippur War had on U.S. military forces. Specifically, it examined the Yom Kippur War to ascertain if American military organizations learned to increase their organizational efficiency and mission accomplishment by analyzing this foreign conflict. This query was a subset of a larger question on how organizations learn and then use those lessons to increase organizational effectiveness and success. Using the organizational history and cultures of the United States Army, Air Force, and Navy the book determined how those factors shaped their respective responses to the Yom Kippur War.

Since Richard Duncan Downie's work on the military as a learning organization began the effort to review the U.S. military services' lessons learned from the Yom Kippur War, it seems fitting that his work help to conclude this book. Downie's theoretical conclusion regarding military learning is short and direct: "militaries innovate without external pressure when they are able to identify external influences that make existing doctrine deficient and achieve consensus on an organizational response to those trends."[1] Organizational resistance to innovation, or change, is due to rigidity in existing doctrine. To avoid such rigidity, Downie argues that organizations need to become learning organizations/institutions. As he stated, "such an institutional orientation is possible, but requires an institutional focus on learning and the development of the structures and procedures necessary to ensure the organization responds effectively to external influences."[2] Downie's analysis is fully consistent with Peter Senge's theory regarding the requirements to become a learning organization.

In the *Fifth Discipline* Peter Senge outlined the criteria for becoming a learning organization. Senge believed a learning organization applies systems thinking and practices personal mastery and lifelong learning. Additionally, a true learning organization uses mental models and questions organizational assumptions, creates a shared vision of the organization, and fosters team learning.³ Throughout this book, Senge's five criteria were used to examine the response of American military services to the Yom Kippur War.

The Yom Kippur War was a relatively short but brutal, high-intensity conflict. The study of the war and its aftermath by the United States strongly influenced the institutions and organizations of the Army and the Air Force. As the book has outlined, that influence is clear when viewed through the lens of Peter Senge's Learning Organization. Tracing the Army and Air Force histories and cultures, the impact of the Yom Kippur War as a major evolutionary and transformational catalyst for both services is evident.

THE U.S. ARMY

Prior to the Yom Kippur War, the United States Army had experienced major organizational trauma from its involvement in the Vietnam War. Many of its internal processes were broken because of the stress the conflict put on its institutions. Thankfully, the Army emerged from the Vietnam conflict with strong leadership that began a coordinated, holistic, and systematic organizational improvement process. General William DePuy and General Don Starry have been highlighted as the most impactful leaders during this transformative period. Even though the post-Vietnam Army had begun its task to reform immediately after the conflict, the Yom Kippur War offered a renewed sense of urgency. The war acted as a real-time battle lab in which the American military could observe and learn truths about the nature of a modern high-intensity conflict. The Army responded eagerly to the lessons of the Yom Kippur War, and comprehensively applied them across its organizational structure.

This book outlined the eight major lessons the Army took away from their evaluation of the war. Because Egyptian and Syrian forces used predominately Soviet military equipment and tactics, the Army determined that any potential conflict with the Soviet Union and Warsaw Pact forces would resemble what unfolded during the Yom Kippur War. That meant the Army would be engaged in a high-intensity battle and incur enormous losses in a short time frame in any war with the Soviets. The Army learned that:

- The use of airpower and air defense systems would be intense,
- No one weapons system would dominate the battlefield,
- Command and control systems would be stretched to their limits,
- More pressure would be brought to bear on leaders to rapidly identify and solve complex situations,
- Initiative would be essential, and

- More intelligence would be required to locate and target enemy follow on forces attacks.

Armed with this information and the impetus to change after the Vietnam debacle, the Army charted a new course.

More than any other service, the Army went about its organizational change systematically, thus demonstrating the characteristics inherent to a learning organization. As the book chronicles, the Army used systems experts from academia to assist this transformation. Changes in personal mastery, mental models, team learning, and shared vision were highlighted throughout the book. One important point discussed in the book is the personal relationships top U.S. Army leaders fostered with key Israeli military officers who had participated in the Yom Kippur War. These close relationships helped the U.S. Army refine the lessons learned from the conflict and inculcate new training and doctrinal procedures into the force.

Internally, the Army changed its training procedures. The construction of a National Training Center (NTC) and investment in new methods and sharpen the skills of its soldiers and leaders, and its doctrinal changes from Active Defense to AirLand Battle are all indicative of the major institutional changes that took place in the service. Additionally, the Army's commitment to five new major weapons systems signaled the importance the institution placed on reshaping organizational capabilities.

The success of the U.S. Army and its adoption of the principles of a learning organization were put on full display during Operations Desert Shield and Desert Storm. The Army that limped out of Vietnam faced one of the largest armies in the Middle East. Using primarily the doctrine of AirLand Battle, the American armed forces devasted the Iraqi military despite their sophisticated Soviet weapons. The successful transformation of the U.S. Army had proven their ability to learn performance-based lessons from another conflict with devastating effectiveness.

US AIR FORCE

The United States Air Force also displayed the characteristics of a learning organization as it negotiated major organizational changes after the Yom Kippur War. Early in its history, the Air Force established a culture of innovation and change as it wrestled with the new technology of manned flight. Organizationally, systems thinking was part of the way it did business. However, the Air Force had its own trauma from its performance in the Korean and the Vietnam Wars.

The Vietnam experience was particularly acute for the Air Force. For example, 395 of the entire fleet of 833 F-105s were lost in Southeast Asia; in fact, the F-105 was withdrawn from combat because of the loss rate.[4] So, the Air Force, like the Army, faced an institutional crisis concerning its ability to perform many of its missions, especially those relevant to the major Cold War theater of record—the Central European region. Once again, the lessons of the Yom Kippur War proved invaluable in influencing the service to adapt its capabilities and procedures in line with that of a learning organization.

As highlighted in the book previously, to gain lessons from the Yom Kippur War the Department of Defense mandated that United States Military Operational Survey Team (USMOST), composed of members from every service, travel to Israel to obtain important information on the conflict. The Air Force also undertook an independent initiative to analyze the results of the war and incorporate lessons learned into its organization. Likewise, the top service leadership pursued meetings with their Israeli counterparts.

In March of 1974, General Robert J. Dixon, Commander of the Air Force Tactical Air Command (where most of the Air Force fighter and attack aircraft resided), met with General Benny Peled, Israeli Air Force Commander, to establish a more professional relationship.[5] Dixon and Peled's ongoing discussions and the ongoing Air Staff analysis drove significant findings for the United States Air Force. Like the United States Army, the Air Force decided to focus on specific areas for the future improvement in its forces. The most impactful lessons to its future success were air superiority, doctrine and training, logistics, and professional military education.

The Air Force systematically worked through these four focus areas. In the realm of personal mastery, the Air Force developed new training venues to hone the skills of its aircrews and support personnel. Establishing the Red Flag facility at Nellis AFB, Nevada, was a critical step in that process. Eventually, captured Soviet equipment from the Yom Kippur War made its way to Nellis and allowed the Air Force to replicate the environment they would face in Central Europe should a conflict with the Soviet Union arise. The Air Force's focus on mental models helped it redefine its doctrine on air superiority. The accumulated Israeli Air Force losses throughout the Yom Kippur War helped the United States Air Force to redefine air superiority and focus on aircraft freedom of action throughout the entire combat theater.[6]

The shared vision with the Army focused on the importance of attritting ground-based air defense systems and helping the Army attack the second and third echelon of Soviet and Warsaw back forces. The formation of the Air Land Forces Application (ALFA) agency and the signing of the Memorandum of Understanding for thirty-one joint initiatives were specific demonstrations of that shared vision. These factors were direct lessons from the Yom Kippur War, which drove the Air Force and the Army toward closer cooperation under the AirLand Battle doctrine.

The Air Force spent considerable effort in team learning as it sought to reinvigorate its professional military education program. The lessons of the Yom Kippur War were prominent throughout Air Force professional military education as it challenged old paradigms and discussed new concepts. Innovative thinkers like Colonel John Warden also used the lessons of the Yom Kippur War to advocate for changes in America's airpower doctrine.

Like the United States Army, the United States Air Force displayed its successful transformation and its use of lessons from the Yom Kippur War during Operation Desert Shield and Desert Storm. The ability of the Air Force to transport and resupply major portions of the American Forces in the Persian Gulf region and its effective attack on Iraqi forces using Stealth aircraft and an integrated air campaign proved devasting to the predominately Soviet-equipped force. There is no doubt that the Air Force demonstrated the characteristics of a learning organization and used the lessons it learned from the Yom Kippur War to great effect.

US NAVY

An analysis of the United States Navy's response to the Yom Kippur War is substantially different than the other services previously examined. The Navy, which has responded to organizational and technological changes throughout its history, found itself in a different space than the Army and the Air Force at the conclusion of the Vietnam War. The Navy fought three related but different wars in Vietnam:

- The ground war via the Marines,
- The air war in the North, and
- The brown water war in the South.[7]

These conflicts did not affect the major mission of the Navy—to control the seas of the Atlantic and Pacific Oceans. Only the air war over North Vietnam provided the Navy the opportunity to derive institutional learning from the experience.

Significant changes to air tactics emerged from the air war that could be applied to the Navy's main areas of concern.[8] This book highlighted the formation of the Navy's Top Gun program which improved the performance of naval aviators during the war. However, as mentioned in the last section, the performance of the Israeli and Arab naval elements during the Yom Kippur War did not involve capabilities or tactics thought to benefit the Navy. The best indication of this is the lack of published literature on the influence of the war on the service, as opposed to the extensive references for the Air Force and the Army. The second indication is the lack of any apparent connection between changes in U.S. naval force structure, weapons systems, leadership, doctrine, or strategies that can be tied to the Yom Kippur experience.

There is a distinct indication that the Marine Corps was able to learn some important lessons from the Yom Kippur War. Taking lessons from Egyptian infantrymen in the Sinai that repelled Israeli armored attacks, the Marines envisioned that infantry properly equipped and trained with anti-tank weapons could deter some armored attacks. Yet, given its limitations to affect the overall budget and doctrine of the Department of the Navy major changes did not occur in doctrinal and organizational factors in the Department of the Navy.

In conclusion, the Navy emerged from the wake of the Yom Kippur War convinced that its method of operations was sound for where it intended to conduct its work—the North Atlantic and Pacific Oceans. One can state that the Navy did not feel it necessary to learn or apply naval lessons from the Yom Kippur War, as the lessons seemed to apply to the littoral maritime domain, one that was not of primary concern to the Navy. The findings from the U.S. military services' learning experiences from the Yom Kippur War are summarized in Table 5.1 below:

Services' Learning Organization Requirements

Learning Organization Characteristics* matched with U.S. Military Services based on actions taken after the Yom Kippur War			
Characteristics	U.S. Military Service		
	Army	Air Force	Navy
Systems Thinking	Yes	Yes	Yes
Personal Mastery	Yes	Yes	Maybe
Mental Models	Yes	Yes	No
Shared Vision	Yes	Yes	No
Team Learning	Yes	Yes	Yes
*From Peter Senge, The Fifth Discipline			

Source: Created by the author, Robert Tomlinson.

NEW INSIGHTS AND OBSERVATIONS

One important observation not covered extensively by Downie or Senge in their discussions about learning organizations is the role of leadership. This may be implied in their studies, but an analysis of the three services gives us important insights into the role that leadership plays in fostering a learning environment. Here particular attention should be paid to the leadership of U.S. Army General Donn Starry. His ability to recognize the problems the Army faced after the Vietnam War and systematically examine paths to performance improvement were remarkable.

There was almost no aspect of Senge's learning organization principles in which General Starry did not play a role. Two important insights regarding Starry's personality traits which were alluded to previously were his ability to persuade others of the importance of his visions, and his skill at working with foreign military officials. His ability to convince the Air Force to adopt his vision of Airland Battle doctrine was critical to the Army's organizational success. Additionally, his ability to befriend foreign military officials, particularly Israeli General Peled, allowed him to gain military insights from the Israelis that would positively impact the United States Army for many years. The Air Force also benefited from important and influential leadership in the form of Generals Dixon, Creech, and Carlton, from Tactical Air Command and Military Airlift Command, respectively. All three of these leaders helped the Air Force as it practiced the disciplines of a learning organization.

Admiral Zumwalt's attempts to change the U.S. Navy's culture and institute some aspects of a learning organization were met with institutional resistance. Organizationally, the Navy felt more comfortable remaining in its existing structure with few doctrinal or structural changes. Again, because the major naval actions of the Yom Kippur War took place in the littorals, the Navy felt no compelling need to institute wholesale change.

The Yom Kippur War offered the Army and the Air Force an unprecedented treasure trove of indirect experience from which they could, and did, learn how to change and innovate. Both organizations did develop the structures, forces, and procedures to take advantage of those lessons. And in the 1990–1991 Operations Desert Shield/Storm, they put all those elements to the ultimate test in combat, and succeeded beyond most peoples' expectations, including their own. However, the global operating environment of the U.S. military services continued to evolve, change, and present different and unique challenges to the services' institutions and organizations.

As Downie pointed out in 1998, and can be extrapolated into recent times, the military services have been far less able to adapt and transform themselves. The services did produce a significant alteration to their doctrines concerning counterinsurgency and stability operations during the time of the wars in Iraq and Afghanistan.[9] However, once the wars wound down, all services have turned away from structures and processes dealing with counterinsurgency and stability to more "comfortable" subjects, like amphibious operations for Marines, air superiority for the Air Force, conventional combat operations (Multi-Domain Battle) for the Army, and blue water operations for the Navy.[10] Even the National Defense Strategy Guidance has downgraded the importance of complex operations (sometimes referred to as Hybrid Warfare).[11] The lack of consensus both among and within the military services, as Downie wrote almost twenty years ago, has continued to inhibit organizational learning in the United States military.

As the United States finds itself in the first quarter of the twenty-first century facing a growing Chinese military capability and a revanchist Russia, what can the United States military services learn in relationship to the Yom Kippur War experience? First, all American military services need to inculcate the principles of a learning organization. This is the best way to capture significant lessons from foreign conflicts and to use those lessons to improve their organizations. Second, America must pay attention to foreign conflicts in which they are not directly involved but offer indications of how our adversaries might fight in the future. The Russian acquisition of Crimea and the Donbass region from Ukraine can certainly give American military leaders insights into new tactics and procedures employed by our potential adversaries. Finally, strong and thoughtful leadership is essential to establish and maintain a learning organization. American military leaders must constantly seek to develop and foster a learning environment within all their organizations. By ensuring that systems thinking, personal mastery, the use of mental models, shared organizational vision, and team learning reside within their organizations, they will provide their organizations the best opportunity to succeed despite the complexities of modern conflict. It is the hope of this author that this book will provide the reader an opportunity to use the example of the American military's response to the Yom Kippur War to gain insight into how they can improve their own learning from future foreign conflicts.

NOTES

1. Downie, *Learning from Conflict*, 243.
2. Downie, *Learning from Conflict*, 243.
3. Peter M. Senge, *The Fifth Discipline: The Art & Practice of the Learning Organization* (New York: Doubleday, 1990), 6–9.
4. Chris Hobson, *Vietnam Air Losses, USAF, USN, USMC: Fixed Wing Aircraft Losses in Southeast Asia 1961–1973* (North Branch, MN: Specialty Press, 2001), 269.

5. Doyle, "The Yom Kippur War" 32.

6. Trevor Cutler, "From Independence to Interdependence: The U.S. Air Force and AirLand Battle, 1973–1985," Thesis unpublished 2015, University of Calgary. 36.

7. Jonathan E. Czarnecki, "Confronting the Enemy: The United States Navy, 1962–1980," in Kenneth Hagan and Michael McMaster, eds. *In Peace and War: Interpretations of American Naval History, 30th Anniversary Edition,* (Santa Barbara, CA: Praeger Security International, 2008), 261–280.

8. The Navy Strike Fighter Tactics Instructor program (TOPGUN) is a direct, tangible, and enduring institutional learning experience from Vietnam. For a good history, consult Robert K. Wilcox, *Scream of Eagles: The Creation of Top Gun and the U.S. Air Victory in Vietnam* (New York: John Wiley & Sons, 1990).

9. See Joint Publication 3–24, "Counterinsurgency" (Washington, DC: Joint Chiefs of Staff, November 22, 2013), and Joint Publication 3–07, "Stability" (Washington, DC: Joint Chiefs of Staff, August 3, 2016).

10. *The 2018 National Defense Strategy* highlights the concept of Dynamic Force Employment which emphasizes the ability of American military forces to engage in major combat operations while having the capacity to respond to lesser contingencies.

11. Department of Defense, "Sustaining U.S. Global Leadership: Priorities for 21st Century Defense" (Washington, DC: Department of Defense, January 2012).

Bibliography

"100 Years of Marine Aviation." *Air and Space Magazine*, (March 12, 2012). https://www.airspacemag.com/military-aviation/100-years-of-marine-aviation-20911884/.

"188th Armored Brigade—Barak." Global Security Org, Israel—188th Armored Brigade—Barak (globalsecurity.org).

"A Brief History of Army Values." https://caccapl.blob.core.usgovcloudapi.net/web/character-development-project/repository/a-brief-history-of-the-army-values.pdf.

"Advantage at Sea: Prevailing with Integrated All-Domain Naval Power." Washington, DC, Department of the Navy (December 2020).

Air Force Historical Support Division. "1949—The Berlin Airlift." https://www.afhistory.af.mil/FAQs/Fact-Sheets/Article/458961/the-berlin-airlift/.

Air Mobility Command Museum. "Operation Nickel Grass." https://amcmuseum.org/history/operation-nickel-grass/.

Alessi-Friedlander, R. Z. "Learning to Win While Fighting Outnumbered: General Donn A. Starry and the Challenge of Institutional Leadership during a Period of Reform and Modernization." In *Military Review* Online Exclusive (April 2017), Learning to Win While Fighting Outnumbered (army.mil).

Amiel, Saadia. "Deterrence by Conventional Forces." *Survival* 20, no. 2 (1978): 58–62. DOI: 10.1080/00396337808441732.

Argote, Linda. *Organizational Learning: Creating, Retaining, and Transferring Knowledge.* New York: Springer Science-Business Media, 2013.

Assessment of the Weapons and Tactics Used in the October 1973 Middle East War. Arlington, VA: Weapons Systems Evaluation Group, October 1974. https://www.cia.gov/library/readingroom/docs/LOC-HAK-480-3-1-4.pdf.

Au-Yeong, S. K. "The Mighty A-4 Skyhawk Was the U.S. Navy's Best Little Bomber." *The National Interest* (October 27, 2015).

Bar-Joseph, Uri. *The Watchman Fell Asleep: The Surprise of Yom Kippur and Its Sources.* Albany, NY: State University of New York Press, 2005.

Blickstein, Irv, et al. *Navy Planning Programing, Budgeting and Execution: A Reference Guide for Senior Leaders, Managers, and Action Officers.* Santa Monica: Rand Corporation, 2016.

"Bombing as a Policy Tool in Vietnam: Effectiveness." In Book 2 *Military Strategy Analysis DS-611*. Maxwell Air Force Base, AL: Department of Aerospace Doctrine and Strategy-Air University, 1988.

Boss, Jeff. "Staying Competitive Requires Adaptability." *Forbes.com*. April 26, 2016. https://www.forbes.com/sites/jeffboss/2016/04/26/staying-competitive-requires-adaptability/?sh=6d77a36c7e6f.

Boyne, Walter. *The Yom Kippur War and the Airlift that Saved Israel*. New York: Thomas Dunne Books, 2002.

"Brief History of the United States Marine Corps." Reference Branch USMC History Division (July 2006). https://www.usmcu.edu/Research/Marine-Corps-History-Division/Brief-Histories/Brief-History-of-the-United-States-Marine-Corps/.

Bronfeld, Saul. "Fighting Outnumbered: The Impact of the Yom Kippur War on the U.S. Army." *The Journal of Military History* 71, no. 2 (April 2007).

Brown, Ian T. *A New Conception of War: John Boyd, the U.S. Marines, and Maneuver Warfare*. Quantico, VA: Marine Corps University Press, 2018.

Brownlee, John C. "Air Bridge to Tel Aviv: The Role of the Air Force Logistics Command in the 1973 Yom Kippur War." *Air Force Journal of Logistics* XV, no. 1 (Winter 1991).

Builder, Carl H. *The Masks of War: American Military Styles in Strategy and Analysis* (A Rand Research Study). Baltimore, MD: John Hopkins Press, 1989.

Burr, William. "The October War and U.S. Policy." Edited by William Burr. In *The National Security Archives*, http://nsarchive.gwu.edu/NSAEBB/NSAEBB98/.

Cantwell, Gregory Lawrence. "From Preamble to Foxhole." PhD diss., University of Kansas, 2010.

Carter, Bradley. "No 'Holidays from History': Adult Learning, Professional Military Education, and Teaching History." In *Military Culture and History* I. Edited by Douglas Higbee. Surrey, England: Ashgate Publishing, 2010.

Central Intelligence Agency. "Intelligence Report: The 1973 Arab-Israeli War: Overview and Analysis of the Conflict." (September 1975).

Central Intelligence Agency. "Soviet Policy and the 1967 Arab-Israeli War." Directorate of Intelligence (March 16, 1970).

Central Intelligence Agency. "The USSR and the Egyptian-Israeli Confrontation." In *Special National Intelligence Estimate*, no. 30–70 (May 14, 1970).

Chapman, Anne. "The DuPuy-Gorman Initiatives." In *The Army's Training Revolution, 1973–1990: An Overview*. Edited by Henry O. Malone and John L. Romjue. Washinton, DC: Center for Military History, 1991.

Chapman, Anne. "The NTC Experience." In *The Origins and Development of the National Training Center*, 81–110. Edited by Henry O. Malone and John L. Romjue. Washington, DC: TRADOC Historical Monograph Series, 2010.

Chapman, Anne. "The Roots of the Concept." In *The Origins and Development of the National Training Center 1976–1984*, 5–12. Edited by Henry O. Malone and John L. Romjue. TRADOC historical monograph series, 1992. https://history.army.mil/html/books/069/69-3/CMH_Pub_69-3.pdf.

"CIA Intelligence Report. The 1973 Arab-Israeli War: Overview and Analysis of the Conflict." (September 1975). https://www.cia.gov/readingroom/docs/1975-09-01A.pdf.

Clodfelter, Mark. "The Limits of Airpower or the Limits of Strategy: The Air Wars in Vietnam and Their Legacies." In *Joint Forces Quarterly* 78 (July 1, 2015). https://ndupress.ndu.edu/Publications/Article/607706/the-limits-of-airpower-or-the-limits-of-strategy-the-air-wars-in-vietnam-and-th/#:~:text=Airpower%20was%20a%20key%20%E2%80%9Cmeans,the%20air%20strategy%20they%20followed.&text=For%20President%20Lyndon%20Johnson%2C%20victory,%2C%20stable%2C%20noncommunist%20South%20Vietnam.

Cohen, Eliot, and John Gooch. *Military Misfortunes: The Anatomy of Failure in War.* New York: Vintage Books, 1991.

Colby, Elbridge, et al. "The Israeli 'Nuclear Alert of 1973': Deterrence and Signaling in Crisis." Center of Naval Analysis [CNA], April 2013. https://apps.dtic.mil/sti/pdfs/ADA579830.pdf.

The Constitution of the United States of America (Article I Section 8, paragraph 12).

Copp, Dewitt S. *A Few Great Captains: The Men and Events that Shaped the Development of U.S. Air Power.* McLean, VA: EPM Publications, 1980.

Correll, John T. "Billy Mitchell and the Battleships." *Air Force Magazine* (June 1, 2008). https://www.airforcemag.com/article/0608mitchell/.

Cristol, A. Jay. *The Liberty Incident: The 1967 Israeli Attack on the U.S. Navy Spy Ship.* Washington, DC: Brassey's Inc., 2002.

Cutler, Trevor. "From Independence to Interdependence: The U.S. Air Force and AirLand Battle, 1973–1985." Thesis unpublished, University of Calgary, 2015.

Czarnecki, Jonathan E. "Confronting the Enemy: The United States Navy, 1962–1980." Edited by Kenneth Hagan and Michael McMaster. In *In Peace and War: Interpretations of American Naval History, 30th Anniversary Edition.* (Santa Barbara, CA: Praeger Security International, 2008.

Davis, Richard G. "The 31 Initiatives: A Study in Air Force-Army Cooperation." Washington, DC: Office of Air Force History, 1987.

Department of Defense. "Sustaining U.S. Global Leadership: Priorities for 21st Century Defense." Washington, DC: Department of Defense, January 2012.

Department of the Navy. "Report of the Air-to-Air Missile System Capability." Review. In *Naval Air System*. Washington, DC: Department of the Navy, January 1, 1969.

Downie, Richard Duncan. *Learning from Conflict: The U.S. Military in Vietnam, El Salvador, and the Drug War.* Westport, CT: Praeger, 1998.

Doyle, Joseph. "The Yom Kippur War and the Shaping of the United States Air Force." Maxwell Air Force Base, AL: School of Advanced Air and Space Studies, Air University, June 2016.

Draft of Report to the Congress of the United States: Airlift Operation of the Military Airlift Command During the 1973 Middle East War, October 10, 1974 logistics Readiness Center IRIS Number 01015859, Air Force History Index.Org.

Fadok, David S. "John Boyd and John Warden: Air Power's Quest for Strategic Paralysis." (Thesis, The School of Advanced Airpower Studies, June 1994).

Farley, Robert. "What If the U.S. Army's 'Big Five' Weapons Programs Had Failed?" In *The National Interest* (July 24, 2020). https://nationalinterest.org/blog/reboot/what-if-us-armys-big-five-weapons-programs-had-failed-165555.

Foreign Relations of the United States, 1969–1976. *Foundations of Foreign Policy*, I, 1969–1972. https://history.state.gov/historicaldocuments/frus1969-76v01/d29.

Futrell, Robert F. "Air Mission Accomplished." Readings Book 2 Military Strategy Analysis DS-611. Maxwell Air Force Base, AL: Department of Aerospace Doctrine and Strategy-Air University, 1988.

Futrell, Robert F. *Ideas, Concepts, and Doctrine: Basic Thinking in the United States Air Force 1907–1960*. Maxwell Air Force Base, AL: Air University Press, December 1989.

Futrell, Robert F. "The Strategic Bombing Campaign." In *The United States Air Force in Korea, 1950–1953*. Washington, DC: Office of Air Force History, 1983.

Goldstein, Lyle J., and Yuri M. Zhukov. *A Tale of Two Fleets: A Russian Perspective on the 1973 Naval Standoff in the Mediterranean*. BiblioGov (November 21, 2012).

Grossnick, Roy A. *United States Naval Aviation, 1910–1995*. Washington, DC: Naval Historical Center, 1997.

Gutfeld, Arnon, and Clinton R. Zumbrunnen. "From Nickel Grass to Desert Storm: The Transformation of US Intervention Capabilities in the Middle East." *Middle Eastern Studies* 49, no. 4 (July 12, 2013): 623–644. DOI:10.1080/00263206.2013.798312.

Hammond, Deborah, and Jennifer Wilby. "The Life and Work of James Grier Miller." In *Systems Research and Behavioral Science*. New Jersey: John Wiley & Sons, Ltd., May 2006. https://doi.org/10.1002/sres.738.

Harris, Phillip R. "Dr. James Grier Miller: Psychiatrist, Scholar, University President, Author. (Obituary)." In *Systems Research and Behavioral Science* 20, no. 3 (May–June 2003). https://go.gale.com/ps/anonymous?id=GALE%7CA102520659&sid=googleScholar&v=2.1&it=r&linkaccess=abs&issn=10927026&p=AONE&sw=w.

Hattendorf, John B. Jr., et al. *Sailors and Scholars: The Centennial History of the U.S. Naval War College*. Annapolis, MD: Naval Institute Press, 1984.

Hattendorf, John, ed. *US Naval Strategy in the 1970s*. Newport, RI: Naval War College Press, 2007.

Haun, Phil. "Peacetime Military Innovation through Interservice Cooperation: The Unique Case of the U.S. Air Force and Battlefield Air Interdiction." *Journal of Strategic Studies*, 2019. DOI: 10.1080/01402390.2018.1557053.

Havron, M. Dean, et al. "Improved Army Training and Evaluation Program (ARTEP) Method for Unit Evaluation." *Study Design & Field Research* Executive Summary, 1. Human Sciences Research, Inc., November 1978.

Headquarters, Department of the Army. *The Soviet Army, Operations and Tactics*—Field Manual 100–2–1. Washington, DC, July 16, 1984.

Headquarters, Department of the Army. *Operations Field Manual*: FM 100–5. Washington, DC: Department of the Army, August 20, 1982.

Helfont, Sam. "Cultural Challenges for Israeli Sea Power in the Eastern Mediterranean." In *Naval War College Review*, no. 1 (Winter 2021).

Heller, Christian. "The Impact of Insignificance: Naval Developments from the Yom Kippur War." *Center for Maritime Security* (February 19, 2019). https://cimsec.org/the-impact-of-insignificance-naval-developments-from-the-yom-kippur-war/.

Herzog, Chaim. *The Arab Israeli Wars: War and Peace in the Middle East from Independence through Lebanon.* New York: Random House, 1983.

Hobson, Chris. *Vietnam Air Losses, USAF, USN, USMC: Fixed Wing Aircraft Losses in Southeast Asia 1961–1973.* North Branch, MN: Specialty Press, 2001.

Human Resources Research Organization. "HumRRO: Who We Are." https://www.humrro.org/corpsite/who-we-are/our-history/.

Kennedy, Gregory C., and Keith Neilson, eds. *Military Education: Past, Present and Future.* Westport, CT: Praeger Publishers, 2002.

Lambeth, Benjamin S. *The Transformation of American Air Power.* Ithaca, NY: Cornell University Press, 2000.

Levey, Zach. "Anatomy of an Airlift: United States Military Assistance to Israel during the 1973 War." *Cold War History* 8, no. 4, October 7, 2008: 481–501. DOI: 10.1080/14682740802373552.

Long, Jeffrey. "The Evolution of US Army Doctrine, From Active Defense to Airland Battle and Beyond." Thesis for Master of Military Art and Science, Ft. Leavenworth, KS, 1991.

Malone, Colonel (Ret.) Dandridge M. "Implementation of the Leadership Goal: A Summary." *Army Organizational Effectiveness Journal*, no. 1 (1985).

Mearsheimer, John. *Conventional Deterrence.* Ithaca, NY: Cornell University Press, 1983.

Mets, David R. "The Air Campaign John Warden and the Classical Airpower Theorists." Maxwell Air Force Base, AL: Air University Press, April 1999.

Montross, Lynn, and Nicholas Canzona. *U.S. Marine Operations in Korea 1950–1953, Volume II. The Inchon-Seoul Operation.* Historical Branch, G-3 Headquarters U.S. Marine Corps, Washington, DC, 1955.

Murray, Williamson. *Military Adaptation in War: With Fear of Change.* New York: Cambridge University Press, 2011.

Musella, Martin. "Air Operations During the 1973 Arab-Israeli War and the Implications for Marine Aviation." Marine Command and Staff College (April 1, 1985). https://www.globalsecurity.org/military/library/report/1985/MML.htm.

National Archives. Vietnam War U.S. Military Fatal Casualty Statistics. https://www.archives.gov/research/military/vietnam-war/casualty-statistics.

Nielsen, Suzanne. *An Army Transformed: The U.S. Army's Post-Vietnam Recovery and the Dynamics of Change in Military Organizations.* The Letort Papers. Carlisle, PA: Strategic Studies Institute, U.S. Army War College, September 2010.

Olmstead, Joseph A., Harold Christensen, and L. L. Lackey. "Components of Organizational Competence: Test of a Conceptual Framework." August 1973. https://files.eric.ed.gov/fulltext/ED080889.pdf.

Orwin, Ethan. "Not an Intellectual Exercise: Lessons from U.S.-Israeli Institutional Army Cooperation, 1973–1982." In *Military Review.* Ft. Leavenworth, KS: Army University Press, January–February 2020.

Peck, Michael. "How the Israelis Shot Down Five MiGs in Three Minutes." In *The National Interest* (April 26, 2018). https://nationalinterest.org/blog/the-buzz/how-israel-shot-down-5-russian-migs-90-seconds-25578.

Rabinovich, Abraham. "The Little-Known US-Soviet Confrontation During the Yom Kippur War." *Global Post* (October 26, 2012). https://www.pri.org/stories/2012-10-26/little-known-us-soviet-confrontation-during-yom-kippur-war.

Rabinovich, Abraham. *The Yom Kippur War: The Epic Encounter That Transformed the Middle East.* New York: Random House, 2004.

Rainey, James C., and Cindy Young. "Maintenance Organization: A Historical Perspective." Edited by James C. Rainey and Cindy Young. In *Old Lessons New Thoughts: Readings in Logistics, History and Technology 2006* (January 2006), 17–34. Maxwell AFB, Gunter Annex, AL: Air Force Logistics Management Agency.

Rasmussen, Richard. "Marine Corps Close Air Support Development From Guadalcanal to Okinawa." (Master of Military Studies Research Paper, Marine Corps Command and Staff, April 2011). https://apps.dtic.mil/dtic/tr/fulltext/u2/a600543.pdf.

Raveh, Saar. "Why Do Militaries Struggle to Learn?" *The Dado Center Journal.* Dado Center for Interdisciplinary Studies. https://www.idf.il/en/minisites/dado-center/vol-8-the-general-staff-part-a/why-do-militaries-struggle-to-learn/.

"Report of the Air-to-Air Missile System Capability." Review, *Naval Air System*, Department of the Navy, Washington, DC, January 1, 1969.

Rich, Ben R., and Leo Janos. *Skunk Works*. New York: Little, Brown and Company, 1994.

Rin, Yoav, and Barry Posen. "Israel's Strategic Doctrine." Santa Monica, CA: Rand Corporation, 1981.

Rodman, David. "Eagle's Eye View: An American Assessment of the 1973 Yom Kippur War." In *Intelligence and National Security Journal* 31, no. 4 (March 5, 2015).

Romjue, John L. *American Army Doctrine for the Post-Cold War.* Washington, DC: Military History Office, 1997.

Schein, Edgar H. *Organizational Culture and Leadership*, 4th Edition. San Francisco: Jossey-Bass, 2010.

Schulz, Martin. "Organizational Learning." In *Companion to Organizations.* Edited by Joel A. C. Baum. Oxford, United Kingdom: Blackwell Publishers, 2001.

Senge, Peter M. *The Fifth Discipline: The Art and Practice of the Learning Organization.* New York: Doubleday, 2006.

Shaev, Aryeh. *Israel's Intelligence Assessment Before the Yom Kippur War: Disentangling Deception and Distraction.* Ontario, Canada: Sussex Academic Press, 2010.

Shazly, Saad El. *The Crossing of the Suez.* San Francisco, CA: American Mideast Research, 2003.

Smith, Dana. "The Air Land Sea Application Center Commemorates 40 Years." In *Air Land Sea Bulletin*, no. 2015–3. Air Land Sea Application Center (July 2015).

Sorley, Lewis. *Press On! Selected Works of General Donn A. Starry* I. Edited by Lewis Sorley. Fort Leavenworth, KS: Combat Studies Institute Press, 2009.

Sorley, Lewis. *Press On! Selected Works of General Donn A. Starry* II. Edited by Lewis Sorley. Fort Leavenworth, KS: Combat Studies Institute Press, 2009.

Speier, William A III. "Operational Art Considerations for Army Air and Missile Defense: Lessons From the October War." Monograph, Ft. Leavenworth, KS: The School of Advanced Military Studies, 2003.

Spencer, John. "What Is Army Doctrine?" West Point, NY: Modern War Institute, March 21, 2016. https://mwi.usma.edu/what-is-army-doctrine/#:~:text=As%20 a%20military%20term%2C%20Army,in%20support%20of%20national%20 objectives.&text=It%20is%20a%20body%20of,the%20Army%20intends%20 to%20fight.

Spiller, Roger J. "In the Shadow of the Dragon." In *In the School of War*. Lincoln, NE: University of Nebraska Press, 2010.

Stewart, Richard W. *American Military History, Volume II: The United States Army in a Global Era, 1917–2008.* Edited by Richard W. Stewart. Washington, DC: Center of Military History-US Army, 2009.

The Gorman Papers. Paul F. Gorman Military Leadership, Collection: Strategy and Tactics for Learning, the Papers of General Paul F. Gorman. https://cgsc.contentdm.oclc.org/digital/collection/p16040coll10/id/99/rec/3.

Tomlinson, Robert. "Airland Battle: A Doctrine for the USAF." Unpublished thesis. Maxwell Air Force Base, AL: Air War College, January 1992.

Toronto, Nathan. *How Militaries Learn: Human Capital, Military Education, and Battlefield Effectiveness.* New York: Lexington Books, 2018.

Tretler, David A. "The Arab-Israeli Conflict: 1967–1979." In *Modern Warfare and Society: Volume II, Military Theory, History, Doctrine and Strategy.* Maxwell Air Force Base, AL: Air Command and Staff College, August 1988.

Trybula, David. "Big Five Lessons for Today and Tomorrow." Carlisle, PA: U.S. Army War College, May 2012. https://apps.dtic.mil/dtic/tr/fulltext/u2/a592510.pdf.

United States Air Force—Air University. "Block VIII: Thinking About War Summary." In *Thinking About War: Military Theory, History, Doctrine and Strategy*, 91–117. Maxwell Air Force Base, AL: Air Command and Staff College, August 1988.

United States Air Force. "Bombing as a Policy Tool in Vietnam: Effectiveness." In Book 2 *Military Strategy Analysis DS-611.* Maxwell Air Force Base, AL: Department of Aerospace Doctrine and Strategy-Air University, 1988.

United States General Accountability Office. "Airlift Operations of MAC During 1973 Middle East War." Report to the Congress of the United States (October 1, 1974), IRIS Public Record K144.054-2V.

United States Marine Corps. "What Is a MAGTF?" United State Marine Corps Official Website (2021). https://www.26thmeu.marines.mil/About/ MAGTF/#:~:text=The%20MAGTF%20was%20formalized%20by,It%20 stated%3A&text=Since%20World%20War%20II%20in,sufficient%20 sustainability%20for%20prolonged%20operations.

"U.S. Marines in Vietnam: 1954–1975." Marine Corps University, Marine Corps University> Research> Marine Corps History Division> Brief Histories> Marines in Vietnam: 1954–1975 (usmcu.edu).

Utz, Curtis. "The Cordon of Steel: The U.S. Navy and the Cuban Missile Crisis." *Naval Historical Center.* Washington, DC: Department of the Navy, 1993.

Wambold, Adam. "Operation Nickel Grass: Turning Point of the Yom Kippur War" (October 8, 2018). https://www.nixonfoundation.org/2014/10/operation-nickel-grass-turning-point-yom-kippur-war/.

Weinland, Robert. "Superpower Naval Diplomacy in the October 1973 Arab-Israeli War." Arlington, VA: Center for Naval Analyses, June 1978.

Wilson, J. R. "US Armor Developments: New Technologies, New Environments, New Concepts." Defense Media Network, November 13, 2014. https://www.defensemedianetwork.com/stories/armor-developments-part-2-new-technologies-new-environments-new-concepts/3/.

Wilson, Jim. "The SR-1 and the Yom Kippur War." *Barnstormers.com*, 77 (August 2009). https://eflyer.barnstormers.com/2009/077-eFLYER-FA02-SR71.html?path=eFLYER/2009/077-eFLYER-FA02-SR71.html.

Wolf, Richard I. "Air Staff Historical Study, The United States Air Force: Basic Documents on Roles and Missions." Washington, DC: Office of Air Force History, United States Air Force, 1987.

Zakheim, Dove. "The United States Navy and Israeli Navy: Background, Current Issues, Scenarios, and Prospects." Arlington County, VA: Center of Naval Analysis (CNA), 2012.

Zisk, Kimberly Maarten. *Engaging the Enemy: Organization Theory and Soviet Military Innovation, 1955–1991.* Princeton, NJ: Princeton University Press, 1993.

Zumwalt, Elmo R. Jr. *On Watch: A Memoir.* New York: Quadrangle/New York Times Books, 1976.

Index

A-4 Skyhawk, 73, 75
Abrams, Creighton, 22, 32
Active Defense, 30, 37; AirLand battle compared to, 31–32; ALFA for, 32
AFLC. *See* Air Force Logistics Command
AH-64 Apache attack helicopter, 30–31
Airborne Warning and Control System (AWACS), 49, 78
The Air Campaign (Warden), 59–60
aircraft carrier, 69–70
Air Force, U.S.: on air superiority, 48, 50–51; in Berlin Airlift, 44; challenges outlined by, 48–50; on critical thinking, 49–50; development of, 43–44, 61n3; Israel supported by, 57–58; in Korean War, 44–46; as learning organization, 47, 61, 87; lessons for, 87–89; on materiel requirements, 49; mental models in, 88; in Offensive Air Support, 33; in Operation Desert Storm, 53, 61, 89; in Operation Nickel Grass, 47; in Operation Vittles, 44; personal mastery in, 88; on PME, 50; prior to Yom Kippur War, 43–47; Red Flag program of, 51, 60, 88; self-evaluation in, 50–61; shared vision in, 32–34, 88; on tactics and doctrine, 49; training centers for, 28; in Vietnam War, 46–47, 87; on Yom Kippur War, 47
Air Force Logistics Command (AFLC), 55, 57–58
AirLand battle, 4n11, 19, 37, 87; compared to Active Defense, 31–32; in Gulf War, 34; shared vision in, 32, 80; Starry on, 32–33, 80
Air Land Forces Application (ALFA) agency: development of, 32, 54–55; doctrine of, 33, 88
air superiority: significance of, 59–60; stealth aircraft and, 53; TAC on, 50–51, 54; Yom Kippur War and, 48
ALFA. *See* Air Land Forces Application agency
Army, U.S.: doctrine for, 28, 30; "How the Army Runs" by, 25–26; in Korean War, 45; lessons for, 86–87; Living Systems Theory used by, 25; mental models in, 28–32; organizational changes in, 20, 87; organizational consensus in, 2; organizational difficulty of, 21; recruiting for, 20, 37n4; shared vision in, 32–34, 37, 88; on Soviet Union, 20; systems thinking in, 25–26; team learning in, 34–37;

training centers for, 27–28; values of, 20; in Vietnam War, 19–20, 86; vision of, 28–29
Army's Training Tests (ATTs), 27
Army Training and Evaluation Program (ARTEP), 27
al-Assad, Hafez, 14
ATTs. *See* Army's Training Tests
Ault report, 70–71
AWACS. *See* Airborne Warning and Control System

Baer, Robert: Starry, Yom Kippur War summary and, 23–26; Yom Kippur War lessons from, 22–23
BAI. *See* Battlefield Air Interdiction
Bar Lev line breech, 13–14
Basic Aerospace Doctrine of the United States Air Force, 54
Battlefield Air Interdiction (BAI), 54
battleship, 68–69, 81n4
Bradley Fighting Vehicle, 30
Brown, George, 32
Builder, Carl, 79

Carlton, Paul Kendall, 56
CAS. *See* Close Air Support
Central Intelligence Agency (CIA), 9
Chief of Naval Operations (CNO), 79
China, 45–46
Chinese Farms attack, 14–15, 17n37
CIA. *See* Central Intelligence Agency
Close Air Support (CAS), 54
CNO. *See* Chief of Naval Operations
Cohen, Eliot, 49–50
Cold War, 3, 4n11, 69–70
Combat Oriented Maintenance Organization (COMO), 52
Constitution, U.S., 68, 81n3
Continental Army Command (CONARC), 20
conventional warfare, 7–8
Cuban Missile Crisis, 69–70
Cutler, Trevor, 47, 58
Czarnecki, Jon, 4n11

Demilitarized Zone (DMZ), 46
Department of the Navy. *See* United States (U.S.) Navy
DePuy, William E., 21, 86; on Army vision, 28–29; doctrine by, 30; on IDF, 26–27, 29; on training, 35
deterrents, 8
Dixon, Robert J., 48, 88
DMZ. *See* Demilitarized Zone
doctrine: Active Defense in, 30–31, 37; by ALFA, 33, 88; *Basic Aerospace Doctrine of the United States Air Force*, 54; FM 100–5, 30–31; M1A1 battle tank and, 31; in organizational learning, 2; of TAC, 52; for U.S. Air Force, 49; for U.S. Army, 28, 30; Yom Kippur War, tactics and, 49. *See also* AirLand battle
Downie, Richard Duncan, 1–2, 85, 91–92
Doyle, Joseph S., 47
Dynamic Force Employment, 93n10

Egypt: Bar Lev line breeched by, 13–14; Israeli conflicts with, 7; naval vessels in, 12–13; in Six Day War, 9; Soviet Union supporting, 9, 11, 15, 73; in War of Attrition, 9; in Yom Kippur War, 11, 14
Eilat, 74
Eskarda Squadron, 72–73

F-105, 88
F-117 Nighthawk stealth fighter, 53
Field Manual (FM) 100–5, 30–31
The Fifth Discipline (Senge), 21, 28, 71–72, 85–86
FM 100–5, 30–31
Forces Command (FORSCOM), 20–21, 36
Furlong, Raymond, 58

General Accounting Office (GAO), 56
Gooch, John, 49–50
Goldwater-Nichols legislation, 71

Index

Gorman, Paul, 24–25, 35
Guadalcanal, 75–76
Gulf War, 34

Hendricks, C. V., 77
How Militaries Learn (Toronto), 1
"How the Army Runs," 25–26
Human Resources Research Organization (HumRRO), 24
Hybrid Warfare, 92

IADS. *See* Soviet Integrated Air Defense System
IAF. *See* Israeli Air Force
IDF. *See* Israel Defense Force
Israel: conflicts with, 7; deterrents used by, 8; on nuclear weapons, 29; in Operation Rimon 20, 10; in Six Day War, 8; strategic depth in, 8–9; U.S. support for, 10, 15, 47, 57–58, 73; in War of Attrition, 9
Israel Defense Force (IDF), 10; DePuy on, 26–27, 29; Israeli Navy and, 74; Latham with, 35; 188th Armored Brigade of, 13; soldier training in, 26–27; TRADOC influenced by, 35; U.S. Marine Corps and, 78
Israeli Air Force (IAF): maintenance structures of, 52; in Operation Rimon 20, 10; in Six Day War, 12; TAC influenced by, 52; in Yom Kippur War, 11, 13–14, 48
Israeli Navy: IDF and, 74; in Six Day War, 12; in Yom Kippur War, 12–13, 74

Janos, Leo, 53
Joint Surveillance Target and Attack Radar System (JSTARS), 33
"Joint U.S. Army and U.S. Air Force Efforts for of Enhancement of Joint Employment of the AirLand Battle Doctrine," 33–34
Jones, David, 72

JSTARS. *See* Joint Surveillance Target and Attack Radar System

Kissinger, Henry, 15
Korean War: Chinese pilots in, 45–46; DMZ established in, 46; U.S. Air Force in, 44–46; U.S. Army in, 45; U.S. Marine Corps in, 76; U.S. Navy in, 70

Lambeth, Benjamin, 46–47
Latham, Willard, 35
leadership: in learning organization, 90–92; in MAC, 91; of Starry, 91; in TAC, 91
Learning from Conflict (Downie), 1–2, 85, 91–92
learning organization: characteristics of, 3–4, 85–86, *90*; leadership in, 90–92; U.S. Air Force as, 47, 61, 87
Liberty, USS, 72
Living Systems (Miller), 25

M1A1 Main Battle Tank, 30–31
MAC. *See* Military Airlift Command
MAGTF. *See* Marine Air and Ground Task Force
maintenance structures, 52
Marine Air and Ground Task Force (MAGTF), 76–77
Marine Corps, U.S.: amphibious capability in, 77–78; aviation in, 45; establishment of, 68, 75; IDF and, 78; in Korean War, 76; lessons learned by, 77–78, 90; Marine Aviation in, 76; Operation Chromite by, 76; in Operation Desert Storm, 78; as separate service, 67; in Vietnam War, 76–77; in World War II, 75–76; in Yom Kippur War, 77
Marten, Kimberly, 2
Mask of War (Builder), 79
McLucas, John, 48
Medium Range Ballistic Missiles (MRBM), 70

Memorandum of Understanding (MOU), 33, 55, 88
mental models, 3; in U.S. Air Force, 88; in U.S. Army, 28–32
Military Airlift Command (MAC), 49; aircraft upgrade for, 56–57; inflight refueling capability of, 56; leadership in, 91; in Operation Nickel Grass, 55–56
military learning: external influences in, 85; impetus for, 2–3; organizational level of, 1–2
Military Misfortunes (Cohen & Goch), 49–50
Military Organizations and Innovation (Marten), 2
Miller, James Grier, 25
Mitchell, Billy, 61n3, 68–69
MOU. *See* Memorandum of Understanding
MRBM. *See* Medium Range Ballistic Missiles
Murphy, Daniel, 72

National Training Center (NTC), 27–28, 87
Naval War College, 80
Navy, U.S.: aircraft carrier in, 69–70; Ault report for, 70–71; battleship in, 68–69, 81n4; in Cold War, 69–70; history of, 68–75; as independent, 71–72, 80; in Korean War, 70; learning inability by, 50, 80, 89–90; littoral waters used by, 80–81; organizational changes in, 68–69; Project Sixty in, 71; Secretary of the Navy in, 67; Senge and, 78–81; in Six Day War, 72; Sixth Fleet of, 72–73; systems thinking lacking for, 71; Top Gun established for, 71, 79, 89, 93n8; tradition in, 79; training centers for, 28; U.S. Constitution on, 68, 81n3; in Vietnam War, 70, 89; in Yom Kippur War, 67, 72–73; Yom Kippur War reviewed by, 74–75

Nixon Doctrine, 20
NTC. *See* National Training Center
nuclear weapons, 21, 29

Offensive Air Support, 33
Office of Strategic Services (OSS), 25
officer's creed, 20
OKEAN 70, 71
Olmstead, Joseph, 24
Operation Chromite, 76
Operation Desert Storm: stealth aircraft in, 53, 61, 89; U.S. Air Force in, 53, 61, 89; U.S. Marine Corps in, 78
Operation Nickel Grass: MAC in, 55–56; U.S. Air Force in, 47
Operation *Rimon 20*, 10
Operation Vittles, 44
organizational competence, 24
organizational consensus, 2
organizational learning, 1; adaptation and, 25; definition of, 2, 4n5; doctrine in, 2; from experiences, 3; in *Military Misfortunes*, 49–50
OSS. *See* Office of Strategic Services
Ostefriesland, 68–69

Patriot Air Defense System, 30
Peled, Benny, 48, 88
Peled, Musa, 34–35, 91
personal mastery, 3; ARTEP and, 27; definition of, 26; TRADOC use of, 26–28; in U.S. Air Force, 88
PME. *See* Professional Military Education
POMO. *See* Production Oriented Maintenance Organization
precision guided weapons (PGMs), 77
Production Oriented Maintenance Organization (POMO), 52
Professional Military Education (PME): air warfare in, 58–59; critical thinking in, 59; purpose of, 58; U.S. Air Force on, 50; Yom Kippur War influence on, 35–36
Project 100,000, 37n4

Project Sixty, 71

Rabinovich, Abraham, 10–11
Raveh, Saar, 2
Red Flag, 51, 60, 88
Rich, Ben, 53
Rodman, David, 78–79

Sa'ar ships, 74
Sadat, Anwar, 9–10, 14
SAMS-3. *See* Surface to Air Missile Systems-3
Schein, Edgar, 25
Schlesinger, James, 48
seam, 14–15, 17n37
Secretary of the Navy, 67
Senge, Peter, 3; *The Fifth Discipline* by, 21, 28, 71–72, 85–86; on shared vision, 32; on systems thinking, 23, 71; on team learning, 34; U.S. Navy and, 78–81
shared vision, 3; definition of, 32; in U.S. Army, 32–34, 37, 88
El Shazly, Saad, 9, 14
Six Day War: CIA report on, 9; Egypt in, 9; IAF in, 12; Israel in, 8; Israeli Navy in, 12; U.S. Navy in, 72
Sixth Fleet, 72–73
Skunk Works, 53
Skunk Works (Rich & Janos), 53
Soviet Air Defense system, 10, 54
Soviet Integrated Air Defense System (IADS), 52, 54
Soviet Union: in Cold War, 69–70; in Cuban Missile Crisis, 69–70; Egypt supported by, 9, 11, 15, 73; Fifth Eskarda Squadron of, 72–73; maritime capability of, 69; nuclear deterrence against, 21; OKEAN 70 by, 71; in Operation Rimon 20, 10; SAMS-3 used by, 10; Syria supported by, 9, 11, 15, 73; U.S. Army on, 20; Yom Kippur War involvement by, 3
Spiller, Roger, 26

Starry, Donn A., 21, 86; on AirLand battle, 32–33, 80; Baer, Yom Kippur War summary and, 23–26; on competence, 24; on FM 100–5, 30–31; leadership of, 91; with Peled, M., 34–35, 91; Yom Kippur War lessons from, 22–23
stealth aircraft: air superiority and, 53; in Operation Desert Storm, 53, 61, 89; of TAC, 52–53
strategic depth, 8–9
Surface to Air Missile Systems (SAMS)-3, 10
Syria: forces of, 12; Israeli conflicts with, 7; naval vessels in, 12–13; Soviet Union supporting, 9, 11, 15, 73; in Yom Kippur War, 11–12
systems thinking, 3; TRADOC use of, 23–24; in U.S. Army, 25–26; U.S. Navy lacking, 71

Tactical Air Command (TAC), 33; on air superiority, 50–51, 54; IAF influence on, 52; leadership in, 91; maintenance structures and doctrine of, 52; stealth aircraft of, 52–53; TRADOC partnership with, 54–55
team learning, 3; continuous learning in, 35; definition of, 34; Senge on, 34; in U.S. Army, 34–37
Top Gun, 71, 79, 89, 93n8
Toronto, Nathan, 1
Training and Doctrine Command (TRADOC): establishment of, 20–21, 36; IDF influence on, 35; personal mastery in, 26–28; systems thinking in, 23–24; TAC partnership with, 54–55
The Transformation of American Air Power (Lambeth), 46
Trefry, Richard, 25–26
Turner, Stansfield, 80
Turner Revolution, 80, 83n55

UH-60 Black Hawk Utility helicopter, 30–31
Ulmer, Walter F., Jr., 25
United States (U.S.), 10, 15, 47, 73
United States Military Equipment Validation Team-Israel (USMEVTI), 75
United States Military Operational Survey Team (USMOST), 22, 48, 74, 88
U.S. Constitution, 68, 81n3
USMEVTI. *See* United States Military Equipment Validation Team-Israel
USMOST. *See* United States Military Operational Survey Team

Vietnam War: U.S. Air Force in, 46–47, 87; U.S. Army in, 19–20, 86; U.S. Marine Corps in, 76–77; U.S. Navy in, 70, 89

Warden, John, III, 59–60, 61, 89
War of Attrition, 9
weapons systems: Big Five in, 30; in Yom Kippur War, 7. *See also* Surface to Air Missile Systems (SAMS)-3
Westmoreland, William, 20
"Why Militaries Struggle to Learn" (Raveh), 2

World War II, 75–76

Yom Kippur War, 1; air superiority and, 48; background for, 7; Bar Lev line breech in, 13–14; ceasefire in, 15, 73; Chinese Farms attack in, 14–15, 17n37; combatants in, 3; Egypt in, 11, 14; IAF in, 11, 13–14, 48; IDF in, 13; initial attack in, 11; Israeli 188th Armored Brigade in, 13; Israeli intelligence site attack in, 11–12; Israeli Navy in, 12–13, 74; learning triggered by, 4; lessons from, 22–23, 92; PME influenced by, 35–36; Starry and Baer summary of, 23–26; Syria in, 11–12; tactics and doctrine in, 49; turning point in, 73–74; U.S. Air Force on, 47; U.S. Marine Corps in, 77; U.S. Navy in, 67, 72–73; weapons systems in, 7
The Yom Kippur War (Rabinovich), 10–11

Z-Grams, 79
Zumwalt, Elmo R.: innovation of, 79, 91; on Project Sixty, 71; reforms by, 80

About the Author

Robert W. Tomlinson is associate professor in the National Security Affairs (NSA) Department of the Naval War College at the Naval Postgraduate School, Monterey, California. He received his BA from the College of the Holy Cross in history. He has a Master's in public administration from Golden Gate University and a Master's in military history and the modern Middle East from California State University at Northridge. He has a PhD in the history of modern Middle East and national security affairs from Claremont Graduate University. Author of *Covering the Shi`a: English Press Representation of Lebanese Shi`a 1975–1985,* prior to his academic career Bob served over twenty-six years in the Air Force as an air battle manager and operational commander, retiring as a colonel.

www.ingramcontent.com/pod-product-compliance
Lightning Source LLC
Chambersburg PA
CBHW020129010526
44115CB00008B/1038